STUDIES IN HISTORY, ECONOMICS AND PUBLIC LAW

Edited by the

FACULTY OF POLITICAL SCIENCE OF COLUMBIA UNIVERSITY

———

Number 573

REPUBLICAN IDEAS AND THE LIBERAL TRADITION IN FRANCE 1870-1914

BY

JOHN A. SCOTT

REPUBLICAN IDEAS ...

AND THE

LIBERAL TRADITION IN FRANCE

1870-1914

BY

JOHN A. SCOTT

1966

OCTAGON BOOKS, INC.

New York

Reprinted 1966
by special arrangement with Columbia University Press

OCTAGON BOOKS, INC.
175 FIFTH AVENUE
NEW YORK, N.Y. 10010

LIBRARY OF CONGRESS CATALOG CARD NUMBER: 66-18043

Printed in U.S.A. by
NOBLE OFFSET PRINTERS, INC.
NEW YORK 3, N. Y.

PREFACE

THE following essay sets forth some of the leading ideas produced by the French republican movement in the period from 1870 until the opening of the first World War, and attempts to trace their origin, evolution and interrelationship. It may be considered as a small contribution to a much larger subject, namely the history of French republicanism from the time of the Great Revolution to the present day.

In this monograph I have tried to show how contemporary political and social thought may be used to illuminate the structure and orientation of the republican movement in the period under consideration. Conversely, I have tried to show that the ideas which men in the past have believed in do not become fully intelligible to us until they are examined in close connection with the other manifold data which history provides. For this reason I have tried to avoid a strictly formal and abstract presentation of the theoretical material.

Many people have helped me in the preparation of this book. In particular it is a pleasure to acknowledge the support of Professors Shepard B. Clough and Jacques Barzun of Columbia University, who have given me the benefit of their advice and criticism at every stage. Mme. Charlotte Muret of Barnard College and Professor Ralph H. Bowen of Columbia have read the completed manuscript, and I am indebted to both of them for valuable suggestions. The work was undertaken under the auspices of the Social Science Research Council, whose grants made possible a year and a half of research both in this country and in France. The staffs of a number of libraries have been of great help to me; in particular I must thank the staff of the Amherst College Library and Mme. Octave Monod of the *Musée Clemenceau* in Paris for their kindness and cooperation. My father-in-law William Haller was of great assistance in seeing the manuscript through the press.

AMHERST, FEBRUARY, 1951.

7

To my Mother and Father

TABLE OF CONTENTS

INTRODUCTION

I

THE concept of republican democracy, insofar as Western European countries are concerned, has found its fullest expression in France. Since the time of the Great Revolution, but especially in the first four decades of the Third Republic, its various elements have received there a richly diversified and systematic formulation. It is the purpose of the following essay to analyse and expound some of the doctrines thus enunciated and to demonstrate their value in connection with the study of French society.

These republican ideas have hitherto received little attention from political scientists. A recent writer has pointed out that "as yet no systematic treatment of the philosophy of democracy has been written;" and has correctly noted that, while much has been done in the descriptive study of democratic institutions, the question of democracy "as a social force, an ethical concept, or a political ideal" has been neglected.[1] This statement is particularly applicable to recent French theory. Much, it is true, has been written about French society during the epoch of the Third Republic. Not a few investigators have chronicled its heroic struggles and petty intrigues, its notable achievements and its transient shames.[2] But as yet the conflicting republican

1 Malcolm M. Willey, "Some Critics and Exponents of the Theory of Democracy," in *A History of Political Theory* (*Recent Times*), edited by Charles Edward Merriam and Harry Elmer Barnes (New York, 1924). This author's criticism is also applicable to the more recently published sketch by Alan F. Hattersley, *A Short History of Democracy* (Cambridge, 1930). This work traces the development of democratic institutions with little reference to the social forces which created them or to the evolution of the ideas that accompanied them. Arthur Rosenberg, *Democracy and Socialism* (New York, 1939), deals in part with democracy as a social force, but this theme is subordinated to a very general sketch of European political history since the Great Revolution.

2 For recent contributions to the history of the Republic see R. A. Winnacker's bibliographical article "The Third Republic, 1870-1914," *Journal of Modern History*, X (1937), 372 ff., supplemented by the list B.1 of the bibliography given below.

theories that both moulded and reflected the profoundest movements of the national life have not been comprehensively
studied.[3] Those theories sprang from revolutionary traditions.
Their precise affiliation with the latter has yet to be traced.[4]

This comparative neglect of the political theory produced
by the republican movement in the period 1870 to 1914 is a
gap in our understanding of France's recent past significant
enough to necessitate some explanation, however tentative, of
its existence. Perhaps the most obvious reason is to be found
in the conditions that prevailed in France between the two

3 F. W. Coker, *Recent Political Thought* (New York, 1934), is described
in the preface (v) as "a review of dominant political ideas, as set forth in
theoretical writings and active social movements, during the period from
about the middle of the nineteenth century to the present day." So far as
France is concerned this work in no way substantiates so ambitious a claim.
E. Kohn-Bramstedt, "Society and Political Thought in France," in *Political
Thought—The European Tradition* (New York, 1939), provides an exceed-
ingly brief survey of French political thought since the Enlightenment,
while R. A. Schermerhorn, "French Political Thought," in *Twentieth
Century Political Thought*, edited by Joseph S. Roucek (New York, 1946),
concentrates upon the period since 1870. Neither of these articles can be
considered a serious contribution to the study of republicanism as the
dominant theoretical trend in the period from 1870 to 1914. Jacob Peter
Mayer, *Political Thought from Sieyès to Sorel* (London, 1943), is an ably
written sketch but does not justify its title.

Of the older works Albert Thibaudet, *Les Idées politiques de la France*
(Paris, 1932), is a pioneer study in its method of showing the connection
between schools of ideas and economic interests, but its usefulness is limited
by the fact that it is only a brief sketch and devotes very little space to the
analysis of strictly republican ideas. Roger Soltau, *French Political Thought
in the Nineteenth Century* (Yale University Press, 1931), deals with republican thinkers but is hampered by too limited an acquaintance with republican
literature in the period after 1870. This author fails to present a picture of
the evolution of republican thought in relation to the life of the time, and
his classification of authors is misleading.

4 The republican ideal and its connection with earlier revolutionary thought
and activity receives brief attention in two recent works by David Thomson,
The Democratic Ideal in England and France (London, 1940), and *Democracy in France: the Third Republic* (London, 1946), but only in a very
general way. Of older works, H. A. L. Fisher, *The Republican Tradition in
Europe* (New York, 1911) and Guido Ruggiero, *A History of European
Liberalism* (New York, 1927), deal only cursorily with the Third Republic.

World Wars. Following 1919 it became very clear that the victory over the Germans for the sake of which the French had made so vast a human sacrifice was a hollow one. It was the prelude not to a hoped-for era of peace but to one of deepening crisis. France fell victim to a series of paralyzing conflicts which reached a climax in the early thirties. Abroad, the rise of Hitler and German fascism demonstrated that hollow victory was being changed into resounding defeat. The Republic found itself menaced by a ring of aggressive dictatorships in Germany, Italy and finally in Spain. At home it was confronted with the rise of a right-wing movement, elements of which drew inspiration and arms from France's authoritarian enemies.

Domestic and foreign crises widened the existing class divisions in French society and thus produced a sickness which expressed itself in a widespread attitude of defeatism and loss of morale. Liberal and democratic ideals, which before 1914 had found, as we shall see, much popularity among the intellectuals, fell into disrepute. True, even before the first World War some republicans, among whom Émile Faguet was the most prominent, had begun to attack the principles of universal suffrage and parliamentary rule upon which French political life was based. But the great conflict of 1914 to 1918 was a major landmark in the evolution and decline of traditional republican beliefs and modes of expression. The generation of scholars and intellectuals that grew up during the war emerged from the experience with troubled minds and shaken convictions.[5] The revolutionary fire of the nineteenth century had vanished in a world dominated by political pigmies and cold intrigue.[6] The older generation, whose ranks still contained many leading figures from the pre-war era, experienced a similar revulsion. They penned diatribes against the stupidity and corruption of

5 Yves Simon, the philosopher, was fifteen years old when the war came to an end. Looking back from the vantage point of 1940 he wrote: " Our life was beginning in an atmosphere of disillusion. Many of us were to become easy victims for the worst forces of nihilism—scepticism, cynicism and despair." *La Grande Crise de la République française* (Montreal, 1941), 18.

6 *Ibid.,* 39.

the regime or sought escape from the present in wistful contemplation of the idealized heroes of the republican past.[7] Too many of France's thinkers and writers thus lost faith in their country's great liberal and revolutionary traditions, or failed to find a way to preserve and carry forward those traditions in a difficult time. It may be understood that their confusion and discouragement did not promote enquiry into the republican past, its beliefs, philosophies and ideals.

So far as political scientists and the scholarly world in general are concerned they have usually identified the political history of the Third Republic, interpreted in the narrowest sense, with the republican movement itself.[8] Historians have filled many books with the largely discreditable account of parliamentary life during the early years of the regime. They have related how the latter, almost as soon as it came into existence, succumbed to the control of business interests and of the clique of politicians who were their political agents. They have shown how the state machinery was used to put through profitable deals, orders and concessions until the word politician became a byword in France for blissful irresponsibil-

7 This nostalgia for the past is illustrated by Daniel Halévy's La Fin des notables (Paris, 1930-1937), a glorification in two volumes of the first decade of the Republic. This author, a member of a celebrated family of liberal intellectuals, expressed his own despair with the present in La Decadence de la liberté (Paris, 1931). He wrote that freedom was not yet dead in France, but was mortally ill. "Our twentieth century," he concluded, "has lost both the concept of liberty and the taste for it." Many other examples of the "literature of disillusion" could be cited. Note especially Hubert Bourgin, Cinquante Ans d'expérience démocratique (Paris, 1925), and Quand tout le monde est roi (Paris, 1930) ; Joseph Barthélemy, La Crise de la démocratie contemporaine (Paris, 1931) ; and Emmanuel Berl, Mort de la pensée bourgeoise (Paris, 1930).

8 The classic illustration of this tendency is to be found in the work of the republican historian Charles Seignobos whose L'Évolution de la Troisième République: 1875-1914, in the series Histoire de France contemporaine edited by Ernest Lavisse (Paris, 1921), is still a standard text. Only three pages out of five hundred are devoted to the intellectual movements of the period. It may be added that this book was designed not as a parliamentary history but as a comprehensive survey of the changing forces in republican life.

ity where the permanent interests of the people were concerned. They have underlined that the regime for these reasons became discredited in the eyes of the masses and at least once in the period preceding the first World War narrowly escaped destruction at the hands of demagogues intent on making capital out of the popular disillusion.

But the French republican movement cannot be limited in this way without obliterating the meaning of the national history of which it is a major expression. This movement was more than the manœuvers of political factions, the itemizing of election results and the recording of scandals. It embraced the main phases, political, social and economic, in the life of the French people. The doctrines produced by the republican movement are an organic part of it and an invaluable aid to whoever wishes to investigate the recent history of France. It is with this in mind that the study of republican theory must be approached.

II

A definition of the term ' republican ' is made difficult by the extreme diversity of the ideas which may be subsumed under it. In this respect all that can be done is to indicate certain characteristics which in the past have been common to republican thought as a whole.

The first and most general characteristic of this type of theory is the advocacy of a republican regime on the grounds that the latter is the antithesis of monarchy and for that reason to be preferred. Belief in the superiority of a republican over a dynastic state is a reflection of the fact that the republican movement, in all its manifestations from the most conservative to the most radical, has been shaped by age-old traditions of resistance to Bourbon absolutism. From the moment when it first became an effective force in politics the French republican movement combated the monarchical principle as an irrational survival of the feudal age, as a buttress of authoritarian ideas and as the political instrument of an obsolete landed aristocracy.

Another characteristic of French republicanism closely connected with the above is the secular spirit which animates it.
Virtually all theory of this type has held that religion is a
purely private concern of the individual and in no way the
concern of the state. It has insisted that the conduct of politics and the education of the citizen must be divorced from
religious influences. This secular attitude, again, reflects the
fact that French republicanism has been shaped by age-old
traditions of antagonism to the Church of France. Under the
ancien régime the latter was one of the principal political allies
of the autocracy, whose power remained virtually intact until
the Revolution of 1789. It controlled a significant portion of
the nation's economic assets and exercized a practically unchal-
lenged authority over the beliefs, the conduct and the education of the people. Republicans have usually regarded the ecclesiastical leadership, or hierarchy, as a stumbling block in
the way of building a democratic society emancipated from the
superstition and obscurantism of the past. To undermine the
social and economic position of the Church and to drive it
out of politics has always been one of the leading objectives
of the republican movement. Thus during the era of the Third
Republic most republicans were able to unite, regardless of their
own personal religious beliefs, on the issue of " the seculariza-
tion of society." In general we may conclude that republicanism
has promoted and reflected a non-religious outlook in which
the profession—if not always the practice—of loyalty to social
ideals has replaced the traditional Christian preoccupation with
the life-to-come.

A further characteristic that lies at the very root of the
republican ideal is the concept of political democracy as organized in the nation-state. The belief that sovereignty is a
permanent and inalienable attribute of the people was developed
historically in France as part of a traditional struggle with the
monarchy from which the other leading ideas of republicanism
have emerged. The concept of popular sovereignty was invoked

as early as the sixteenth century by both Catholics and Protestants to justify resistance to the pretensions of the Crown and to provide a sanction for the imposition of constitutional checks upon royal authority. It is true that not all those who made appeal to popular rights and interests accepted the full implications of their position. During the Great Revolution, for example, the constitutionalists appealed to popular sovereignty as the justification of the *bourgeois* parliamentary Assembly, but sought nonetheless to limit the powers of representative institutions, to restrict the electorate and to devise a system of checks and balances that would protect legislatures from what they considered to be excessive popular pressure. The republicans alone followed the idea of popular sovereignty to its logical conclusion. They rejected constitutional or limited monarchy and demanded that the recognition of at least the theoretical supremacy of the people as expressed through a broad suffrage should become the basis of the state. From that day to this the twin concepts of republic and of political democracy have remained inseparably linked in the French mind.

A final element that characterizes most republican thought is a deep speculative and practical concern with the social question. French republicanism, at its first appearance, was a specific product of the Revolution of 1789. It provided an immediate solution for a number of urgent problems raised by the actual unfolding of the revolutionary movement. But the latter was coincidental with the beginnings in France of modern machine and power technology. Republican thought during the nineteenth century developed *pari passu* with the development of industrial capitalism. It was hence inescapably concerned with the conflicts to which the latter gave rise. Class conflict, it is true, is almost as old as human society itself, but this secular reality now assumed a radically new form in the clashing interests of the industrial workers and their masters. In this form it became a force that clearly dominated society and its perspectives.

Republican thought has been preoccupied with this question. All republicans have recognized class war as a profoundly disruptive social force, but their reactions to the problem have been extremely diverse. Proposals for the abolition of class conflict have been put forward that range from devices to bring about social peace and class reconciliation to advocacy of the ideals of socialism and a classless society. Since the Great Revolution the republican movement has produced much penetrating criticism of the capitalist order and many programs for its abolition or reform. From the very beginning the word ' republic ' has represented to millions of Frenchmen a social as much as a political ideal.

Such are some of the complex associations of republicanism in the minds of the French. During the great historical conflicts which have attended France's entry into the modern era this many-sided ideal has evoked and reflected social movements endowed with volcanic energy. It has helped to throw up the barricades and inspire the battles from which French democracy has grown and drawn its strength.

The republican movement whose general characteristics have been sketched above triumphed in France during the last quarter of the nineteenth century. Some historians of this movement have advanced the view that it was a phenomenon of only very recent growth and that its historic traditions, its connections with the past, were negligible. It has been asserted that republican democracy sprang, as it were, fully armed from French soil at no earlier a time than the end of the eighteenth century. James Bryce, for example, that celebrated and influential student of political institutions, was of the opinion that France " adopted democracy by a swift and sudden stroke, without the long and gradual preparation through which the United States and England and Switzerland passed, springing almost at one bound out of absolute monarchy into the complete political equality of all citizens." [9]

9 *Modern Democracies* (New York, 1921), I, 208. To a more recent student, David Thomson, the republican and revolutionary traditions are

If the study of French republicanism is approached from this point of view its leading characteristics are likely to be misunderstood and misinterpreted. It is true that the republican form of government appeared in France with startling suddenness for the first time during the Great Revolution, and it is true that republican thought hardly made its appearance in France before the advent of the nineteenth century. But it would be quite mistaken to conclude for these reasons that republican theory had no preparation in the past; that under the absolute monarchy the ground had not been prepared, intellectually, socially, economically for the achievement of democratic institutions. A strong case, indeed, might be made for the contention that modern French republicanism sprang from a liberal and democratic tradition which is to be traced back as far as the Reformation, if not further. It might be pointed out that the leading elements in what was to become republican thought had been developing in France for many years before the Revolution, and that these elements were not generated spontaneously within the womb of monarchical society but were themselves the expression of generations of struggle against absolutism. It might be pointed out that the social movement of which the French Reformation was itself a product was of great significance in establishing a tradition of national struggle against the feudal and ecclesiastical aristocracy, against the Church and the monarchy.

But the elaboration of such a position would take us far afield. The revolutionary tradition to which the struggles of the sixteenth century gave rise was decisively checked with the triumph of absolutist monarchy in the succeeding period. The first tentative formulations which that tradition had received at the hands of *bourgeois* and Huguenot theorists like François Hotman, Jacques Bretagne and Philippe Duplessis-

---

synonymous. Their starting point, he considers, is the year 1789. The revolutionary tradition, he says, "... had become dissociated completely from the traditions of the ancien regime, ..." *Democracy in France, op. cit.*, 15.

Mornay were not elaborated further. France had to wait until almost the dawn of the eighteenth century before the rationale of revolutionary action against an oppressive Crown could begin to be articulately and systematically set forth. Thus the tradition from which French republicanism sprang received its classic formulation during the Enlightenment. It is true that this formulation was influenced in many important ways by the prior writings and struggles of the French Protestant movement, but it constituted in itself the starting point for fresh and more comprehensive revolutionary struggles against the Crown. The Enlightenment built up a *corpus* of political theory which was its chief glory and no small a contribution to the cause of human progress.[10] To it modern republican thought is bound by close links and owes an immeasurable debt. This theory made a majestic tally of the crimes to be laid at the door of Church and Crown, indicted in Promethean tones the existing regime and tentatively sketched the bases of a more rational social order. In so doing it defined the tradition which forms the starting point of modern republican thought. To the main elements of this tradition some attention must now be given.

The first great element in the modern republican outlook that received elaboration during the Enlightenment was the conception of the rights of man. The liberals of those days were either members of the middle class or of the progressive nobility. They wished to see the monarchy reformed and the worst of its excesses pruned away, but in no sense did they desire the overthrow of the throne itself, for that, they considered, would presage universal anarchy. And yet they formulated a bill of civic liberties whose terms are at the very root of later republican ideals. They elaborated a concept of man as a being

10 Carl Becker, in his lectures entitled *The Heavenly City of the Eighteenth Century Philosophers* (New Haven, 1932), reduced the activities of the *philosophes* to a mere intellectual shadow-play. It is necessary to take issue sharply with this nihilistic interpretation. The *philosophes* were clearly thinkers and publicists who penned a valid indictment of decadent feudal society and pointed the way to a more rational order.

with certain inalienable rights which underlies most later developments in France of the idea of political democracy.

In formulating their creed of political equality the thinkers of the Enlightenment were greatly influenced by the writings of John Locke. Locke had taught that men were born, and must remain, free and equal, and that they possessed certain fundamental rights which no government might legitimately take away. This conception was charged with significance for the history of the English-speaking world, but it also received a classic elaboration in France. If the immediate stimulus for this type of thought came from abroad it quickly took root in French soil and bloomed like a native plant. French eighteenth century theorists of the rights of man were in fact resuming a tradition that had been established mainly by Protestants in the two preceding centuries. These men had taught that there were certain human rights recognition of which must form the basis of secular rule. Violation of these rights by the ruler entitled men, if necessary, to have recourse to force.[11]

The Enlightenment's most comprehensive statement of human rights was made by Voltaire. Freedom, he wrote, was a civic state that resulted when the laws protected all men equally. In a free state all men without exception would be subject to laws consecrating the " natural rights " of humanity. Voltaire conceived that these rights might be ascertained by following the dictates of common sense and by consulting the people themselves. In his opinion they included the freedom of each to dispose of himself and his property as he would, freedom of speech and press, freedom from arbitrary trial and punishment, freedom to profess the religion of one's choice and, above all, freedom of thought.

The revolutionary nature of such teaching in an age of absolute and arbitrary monarchical rule can hardly be over-

11 Jean Fabre, *Les Pères de la Révolution* (Paris, 1910), 37. For a brief account of the ideas of Hotman and Duplessis-Mornay, see Georges Weill, *Les Théories sur le pouvoir royal en France pendant les guerres de religion* (Paris, 1891), chapter 5. Jurieu's leading ideas are clearly set forth in Henri Sée, *La Pensée politique en France au 17ᵉ siècle* (Paris, 1923), 201 ff.

emphasized. Many other thinkers echoed and developed the program which the sage of Ferney voiced so comprehensively. Further attention may well be given to a more detailed account of these special contributions to the eighteenth century creed of equality.

Personal freedom was a concept central to this creed. This idea came to possess significance in part by reason of the vehemence with which the *philosophes* attacked the institution of slavery.[12] Montesquieu in particular addressed himself to this question. If, said he, men were by nature equal, then slavery was contrary to nature. The freedom of each was part of the freedom of all, and none could be wholly free while some remained in chains.[13] Montesquieu specifically assailed Catholicism for asserting its right to reduce to slavery those who did not profess the Catholic religion, as shown by the way in which French and Spanish colonizers treated the Negroes and aborigines in the New World. The Catholic defense of this practice, he said, was the blasphemy of brigands who attempted to hide their crimes under a mask of holiness.

In Voltaire's hands Montesquieu's attack on slavery was widened and made to apply to the semi-servile status of the mass of the French peasantry. Serfdom, it is true, had become the exception rather than the rule in eighteenth century France, but the peasant's property was burdened with a mass of obligations, taxes and dues which survived from the feudal period and still constituted the economic basis of the aristocracy's power.[14] The majority of farmers still followed a miserable,

12 Slavery, it must be remembered, continued in those days to be practised not merely in France's overseas colonies and plantations, but in the mother country itself. Until quite late in the eighteenth century it continued, in the form of galley-service, to be used as a punishment for recalcitrant Protestants who refused to accept the Catholic faith.

13 It is a measure of Montesquieu's perspicacity that this doctrine became an axiom of nineteenth and twentieth century liberal thought. His views on slavery will be found in *Esprit des lois*, Book XV.

14 For feudal survivals and the incidence of serfdom in the eighteenth century see Henri Sée, *Esquisse d'une histoire économique et sociale de la*

poverty-ridden life in which they provided most of the wealth of the state and derived the least benefit from it. Applied to the French peasantry, therefore, the conception of slavery as an unnatural and degrading condition became a rallying cry for the abolition of the *ancien régime* itself and for the creation of a fully emancipated citizenry.

It would have been illogical if the thinkers of the Enlightenment, championing physical freedom, had not championed intellectual freedom too. One of the earliest of these defenders of freedom of thought was Pierre Bayle. Bayle, the son of a Protestant minister, threw over religion in his youth and adopted the position of freethinker, rationalist and sceptic. His forefathers as heretics had claimed the right to read the Bible freely. Bayle went beyond this position and claimed for men the right to read anything they chose, whether of a religious nature or not.[15] He taught that persecution of ideas was unjustifiable and that every man had the right to adopt and adhere to those opinions which seemed to him to be most reasonable. In the hands of Voltaire and Condorcet this doctrine became part of the very core of eighteenth century political egalitarianism and of its liberal tradition.

The human right which the *philosophes* defended in greatest detail and with the most vehemence was the right to freedom of conscience and to freedom of worship.[16] Numerous thinkers

---

France (Paris, 1929), 216 ff.; and Jean Jaurès, *La Constituante*, vol. I of the series *Histoire socialiste de la Révolution Francaise*, edited by Jean Jaurès (Paris, Mathiez edition, 1939), I ff.

15 "Bayle," as Fabre has well pointed out, "is the link between the fathers of the Reformation and the fathers of the Revolution." *Op. cit.*, 7.

16 This view is opposed to that taken by R. M. MacIver, who has written: "When every other method failed governments were driven to admit that citizenship need not demand a particular confession of religious faith. The admission was pragmatic, for even the leading thinkers of the eighteenth century, including Rousseau and Burke, could not accommodate it to their philosophy of the State." *The Web of Government* (New York, 1947), 134. MacIver's position could be refuted by an examination of the work of many eighteenth century writers. Bayle, for example, defended absolute freedom

urged that religious sects should be tolerated regardless of creed, or that all religions should be placed upon the same footing in relation to the state. Even before the beginning of the eighteenth century Archbishop Fénelon and Pierre Bayle had directed their fire at persecution for conscience' sake. Montesquieu attacked intolerance in his *Lettres persanes* with weapons of sarcasm and wit. Voltaire devoted his life to warfare against the mental savagery that led men to destroy minorities for the sake of their beliefs. But the earliest systematic formulation of the right to unfettered freedom of conscience was made by Anne Turgot. His teaching, elaborated by Honoré de Mirabeau [17] and Condorcet, was driven to its logical conclusion during the Revolution in the disestablishment of Church and state and the recognition of the legal equality of all sects.

Turgot [18] based his opinions on the strictly primitive Christian and Protestant conception of a religious community. The Church, he said — his remarks referred specifically to the Catholic Church, but may be taken as having general significance—was a community of believers. Concerned not with the world but with spiritual salvation it must not resort to force in order to maintain its dogmas or to extend its authority. Its only means of proselytizing should be by persuasion. Ecclesiastical sanctions should be only spiritual; rebels or dissidents, that is, should be punished by nothing more than excommunication and similar non-material measures. Religions,

---

of thought in principle. The only limitation that he admitted was the necessity to ban the expression of ideas that constituted direct incitement to commit crimes against society, such as murder, arson and theft. He specifically defended the civil rights of atheists. Equally radical, and equally principled, was the teaching on this question of Meslier, Turgot and Condorcet, to name but three among many.

17 " Unlimited freedom of worship," wrote Mirabeau, " is so sacred a right that the word *toleration* used in this context itself smacks of the tyrannical." Quoted by Fabre, *op. cit.*, 117.

18 Turgot's doctrines of freedom of conscience were first developed in two " Letters on Toleration," written in 1752 and 1753, and in " The Conciliator, or Letters of an Ecclesiastic to a Magistrate," 1754. *Œuvres de Turgot* (Paris, 1844), II, 675 ff.

he went on, were not entitled to any kind of special protection and they ought to exist without being accorded a privileged position in society. All that they were entitled to ask was the right to live, teach and worship in undisturbed freedom. Conversely, the state had no right to adopt a given religion arbitrarily. Religion was, and must remain, a practice founded upon individual conviction; its essence was the right of men to choose freely and to adhere to those beliefs which they felt were true and offered them the surest path to salvation. While a king had the right to belong to a church, he exercized this right as an individual, and not as a ruler. It was not for him to prescribe to his subjects the kind of worship that they should adopt. But Turgot did not feel that the state should for this reason abdicate all right to protect religion; while advocating the disestablishment of the Gallican Church, he nevertheless feared the growth of irreligion, immorality and superstition among the masses. These evils might, he thought, be combated by the erection of a state-endowed cult of 'natural' religion, which would assume responsibility for public instruction and the inculcation of godliness. Nor was this position inconsistent at a time when virtually all public education was in the hands of the Church; Turgot was, in fact, suggesting that the state should organize civic education, and that this function should be divorced from the propaganda of any particular creed. Inculation of 'natural' religion as thus understood was entirely compatible with the advocacy of radical disestablishmentarianism. " I would wish," he wrote, " that the state should do *nothing else* for this religion but to ensure its permanence by instituting a regular system of public instruction, organized in all parts of the country and within reach of all citizens." [19]

Along with the rights of man the *philosophes* developed a concept of popular sovereignty that came to form a central element of the Enlightenment's liberal creed. The Huguenots, it is true, had contended many years before that the purpose of government should be to promote the welfare of the people.

19 *Œuvres, op. cit.*, II, 677. Italics not in the original.

But their thinkers were men of noble or *bourgeois* origin who wished to limit the pretensions of the Crown by subjecting the latter to the control of the Third Estate. For this purpose they invoked popular sovereignty as the sanction for a parliamentary regime, but they hesitated to push too far an ideological weapon that might conceivably at some future date be used against themselves. Seventeenth century Protestant thinkers did not find it inconsistent, even while maintaining the above position, to teach that government was sacrosanct and that the king as ruler of the state was the servant of God.[20]

The terrible persecutions which culminated in the Revocation of the Edict of Nantes in 1685 provided a fresh stimulus for the elaboration of a consistent theory of popular sovereignty. Jurieu, one of the most distinguished of the band of French Protestant refugees in Holland, wrote in 1688 that the people had the right to choose their own form of government and that government itself depended upon popular consent.[21] He taught that the people were the ultimate source from which political sovereignty was derived, and that they alone conferred sovereignty upon a ruler. But like his predecessors Jurieu found it difficult to emancipate himself from the idea that political authority, once conferred upon a ruler, could not be revoked. He insisted that when the people had granted power to a ruler they could not resume it at will. But he did believe that sovereignty in order to remain legitimate must be exercized in conformity with " natural rights " and for the purpose of promoting the general interest. This principle, he considered, would be a sufficient guarantee against the degeneration of legal into arbitrary rule.

In some way, not further explained, Jurieu believed that supreme power even when delegated to a king still continued

20 Sée, *Idées politiques, op. cit.*, 193, and Guy Howard Dodge, *The Political Theory of the Huguenots of the Dispersion* (New York, 1947), 5 ff.

21 The most recent treatment of Jurieu's political theory is to be found in Dodge, *op. cit.* See also Paul Pic, *Les Idées politiques de Jurieu et les grands principes de '89* (Montauban, 1907).

to reside in the people themselves. In the eighteenth century this idea made rapid forward strides. The doctrine of natural rights, tentative and qualified assault on royal power as it was, was complemented as a weapon against absolutism by the full and logical development which popular sovereignty received at the hands of Jean-Jacques Rousseau. Rousseau taught that sovereignty was an attribute of the community and could not possibly be alienated by it either temporarily or permanently. Government with its various specialized functions was merely an instrument for the expression and execution of the popular will. Legislators and administrative officers were no more than public servants who held their positions at the pleasure of the people, and were to be appointed and recalled as the latter saw fit.[22]

Rousseau considered that the ideal form of government was a republic as embodied in the city-state of the Ancient World. He found himself in a political dilemma because he considered that the necessary conditions for really democratic rule did not exist in the large centralized state of modern times.[23] This led him into truly absurd paradoxes, such as advising the Poles to dismember their country and the Corsicans to abolish the coinage. Yet Rousseau's doctrine of sovereignty was a revolutionary one. It transformed the liberal creed of the Enlightenment and profoundly influenced all subsequent republican thought.

The doctrine of natural rights which Locke and his French disciples had been at such pains to develop was of little consequence to Rousseau. Laws, he taught, were the condition of

22 This conception of the state as the servant of the people and the agent of their welfare was also developed by the utilitarians Helvetius and d'Holbach. In their view the state's function was to promote communal happiness as measured by the promotion of pleasure and the avoidance of pain. The art of legislation consisted in deciding what measures would ensure maximum happiness and of enacting them to the accompaniment of suitable sanctions in the shape of rewards and punishments. On the utilitarian view the people had the right to change their government if the latter on balance achieved more harm than good.

23 See below, 33.

civil life, and those who obeyed them should be the authors of them.[24] If this were so, no limits could clearly be placed upon the people's power to legislate as they saw fit. Locke's conception of natural rights and Rousseau's of unlimited popular sovereignty were in fact diametrically opposed. Both were incorporated into the Enlightenment's political creed. This was to be a fertile source for future conflict, but the combination of opposites was also to be of great significance in the French liberal tradition. A broad and humane program of civil rights and a clear-cut logical doctrine of popular sovereignty, such were its central achievements in the eighteenth century.

A brief reference, finally, must be made to the social criticism of the *philosophes*, as opposed to their political theorizing. The Enlightenment was characterized by a luxuriance of ideas on the theme of social equality. Scarcely a writer of note, no matter how moderate his views, failed to call attention to the unjust distribution of wealth and to all the evils that flowed from it.[25] This type of criticism put the *ancien régime* in a harsh light, but it must be noted that the critics showed little or no disposition to challenge the institution of private property. Eighteenth century philosophy was almost unanimous in agreeing with the Physiocrats that private property was itself an inalienable right. Indeed the social egalitarian writing in which this period abounded is very far from having the ' socialist ' implications that have sometimes been ascribed to it.[26] In gen-

24 " Du contrat social," in *The Political Writings of Jean-Jacques Rousseau*, edited by C. E. Vaughan (Cambridge, 1915), II, 50.

25 Direct attack upon existing property relations was, at that time, rarely resorted to. In order to sidestep the censorship writers preferred to approach the subject obliquely. They resorted to such devices as the description of ideal commonwealths or the relation of (imaginary) travellers' tales. In this way they were able to contrast existing injustices with utopian situations where better conditions were conceived to prevail. The richness of this egalitarian theme is illustrated by André Lichtenberger, *Le Socialisme au 18ᵉ siècle* (Paris, 1895).

26 Lichtenberger, *op. cit.*, is a case in point. The title of his work is very misleading. It deals with expressions of social egalitarianism in the eighteenth century, not with socialism, a word whose connotations were unknown to the Enlightenment.

eral it limited itself to attacking feudal forms of taxation and of ownership and to demanding the abolition of anachronistic rights and privileges. Only very rarely, as in the writings of Jean Meslier and of the *Abbé* Morelly [27] did the assault on feudal property pass over into a critique of property in general. But this early social criticism did exert, primarily through François-Noel Babeuf, no small influence upon the course of the Revolution. It both foreshadowed and stimulated the development of social thought during the nineteenth century. The Enlightenment contributed little that was positive in the way of coherent social doctrine, but to its inspiration the social thought of the later republican movement was to remain heavily indebted.

III

The anti-authoritarian tradition of the Enlightenment did not arise, as it were, out of a void. It generalized the principles and objectives of the struggle against absolutism and feudal survivals in which the entire French people found themselves engaged. The impressive intellectual activity of the eighteenth century would have been devoid of meaning had it not been more or less directly related to the transformations then occurring in French society. At a time when reviving industry and commerce were accelerating the dissolution of the old order the theorizing of the *philosophes* placed sharp weapons in the hands of the mercantile interests. The Great Revolution broke out when the latter found occasion to challenge the domination of the state by the Crown and aristocracy.

In the first phase of the Revolution many of the demands of the *philosophes* were written into law. The curbing of absolutism in the name of popular sovereignty, the destruction of the secular power of the Church and the granting of civil rights

27 In his *Basiliade* and *Code de la Nature* Morelly described an ideal commonwealth based upon common ownership and cultivation of the soil. Jean Meslier voiced the same idea earlier in the century in his *Testament*, but neglected to develop it.

to all composed the principal work of the Constituent Assembly
that sat from 1789 to 1791.

The early Church settlement was made under financial pressure of the most practical sort, but the influence of the *philosophes* may clearly be seen in the new system that was established. The revolutionaries followed Turgot in attempting to weaken the secular power of the Church while leaving its spiritual authority over the masses undiminished. The very decree that declared all Church property to be at the disposal of the nation established the principle that public worship and the support of ministers were state responsibilities. Ecclesiastical lands were confiscated and monastic orders dissolved *pari passu* with the transfer to the state of authority over the Church organization. Toleration for other than Catholic beliefs was given grudgingly at first [28] but a decree of 1791 established full liberty of worship, and the Constitution of the same year guaranteed to all the right to exercise freely the religion of their choice. Ecclesiastical buildings were made available for the use of all sects, and the registration of births, marriages and deaths, for centuries past the prerogative of the Church, was declared a civic function.[29] By such measures as these the secular power of the Church was drastically diminished and its age-old spiritual monopoly was ended.

The influence of the *philosophes* was manifested with similar decisiveness in the famous Declaration of the Rights of Man which the National Assembly adopted in 1789.

As far as the principle of popular sovereignty was concerned the revolutionaries at first took only the most cautious steps. The eighteenth century *bourgeoisie*—and the Third Estate in the Assembly of 1789 was composed principally of its representatives—had the most limited political aims at the start. It sought an accommodation with the King and the aristocracy.

28 " No one," the Declaration of the Rights of Man proclaimed, " is to be molested for his opinions, even his religious opinions, providing that their manifestation does not disturb public order as established by law."

29 Alphonse Aulard, *Christianity and the French Revolution* (London, 1927), 91.

The idea of destroying the Crown, driving out the nobility and assuming a monopoly of state power was very far from its thoughts, though after 1792 it was compelled to do all these things. The *bourgeoisie* wished at first to establish a constitutional monarchy on the English model, and it gave expression to this purpose in the Constitution of 1791. The latter provided for a single-House Assembly which would in the name of the people control and limit royal authority, not sweep it away. But the Assembly itself was based upon high property qualifications for both electors and candidates. It was in no sense intended to be a product of universal suffrage or a Rousseauan representative of the people's will.[30]

By 1791 the liberal ideas and traditions of the *philosophes* were enshrined in the most moderate of state settlements. It was to be a fact of the most far-reaching significance for the course of French history that even this was repudiated by the monarchy. The king and the court refused to accept the 1791 Constitution. The upper clergy, imbued with aristocratic sympathies, rejected it. Both sides welcomed war as a way out of the impasse,[31] but this intensified the political crisis. The revolutionaries were driven by the force of circumstances to go far beyond their original purpose and to destroy the monarchy itself. Republicanism made its first appearance in France as the expression of the eighteenth century tradition of civil rights, popular sovereignty and the lay state. *From that day to this these traditions and the republican state-form have remained inseparably linked in the minds of the French.*

The First Republic was inaugurated on September 22, 1792. It waged war at home against federalists and Vendeans, against aristocrats and priests. It swiftly organized armies and drove the German invader from French soil. The republicans of those

30 The Constitution of 1791 is lucidly analyzed by Alphonse Aulard, *The French Revolution* (New York, 1910), vol. I.

31 The economic factors that precipitated the war are dealt with by Daniel Guérin, *La Lutte de classes sous la Première République* (Paris, 1946), I, 46 ff.

days won fame by their deeds, but they acted largely in re-
sponse to the needs of the moment and hardly at all in accordance with clearly defined principles. For this, of course, there
were sufficient reasons. The Enlightenment had prepared men's
minds for revolutionary change and had sketched in general
terms the political bases upon which the new *bourgeois* order
might be built. But it furnished no tactical guide for the many
problems raised in the course of the Revolution itself. The early
republicans were not always sure what their objectives were
nor how they should achieve them. To a large extent republicanism at its first appearance in France was theoretically incoherent.

The concept of the word ' republic ' which was current at
the end of the eighteenth century is an example of the imma-
turity of contemporary thought on that subject. The *philosophes* had little first-hand knowledge of republics and less
grounds for generalizing about them: [32] their books might be
ransacked in vain for any guidance on the question whether a
republic should be instituted in France and of what it should
consist. On this issue eighteenth century theory remained
dumb. The *philosophes* discussed governmental reform at
length and dwelt upon the types of government which might
be favorable to the progress and elevation of mankind. The
alternatives to which they gave most attention were despotism,
representative government of the English or Venetian type,
and direct republican democracy. These alternatives were described and commented upon, but no conclusion was reached
as to which was the most desirable. Thinkers as widely opposed
as Montesquieu and Rousseau would have agreed that the form
of government cannot be fixed once and for all for a given
society, but must remain responsive to changing social con-

32 Switzerland, Venice, and the United States of America were the outstanding contemporary examples. Many of the *philosophes* had an extensive
knowledge of the Greek and Roman republics in the ancient world. For the
role of antiquity in the formation of Montesquieu's ideas, for example, see
Lawrence Meyer Levin's *The Political Doctrine of Montesquieu's Esprit
des Lois: Its Classical Background* (New York, 1936).

ditions. At certain times, for certain peoples, the *philosophes* would have agreed, a republican regime would be appropriate.

Enlightened despotism presented little difficulty to the men of the eighteenth century; numerous examples could be cited where absolute monarchs had themselves initiated the social reforms so ardently championed by the *philosophes*.[33] Under some conditions, also, representative government appeared to be equally successful in promoting enlightened rule. In England, where a narrow aristocratic and commercial oligarchy shared political power, institutions existed—such as the jury system, or freedom of the press—which were the wonder of all Europe. But the democratic republic, in which the whole people, as opposed to a mere oligarchy, made the laws, was a form of government that troubled the theorists. Voltaire, Montesquieu, and Rousseau, who appreciated the value of this type of regime in the ancient city states, were unable to see how it could be adapted to modern conditions. It was the essence of real, direct democracy, thought Rousseau, that the people's will could not be represented by delegates or assemblies, but must be exercised in person by all the members of the state. If this was true, clearly democracies must always be small enough to permit all the citizens to meet together in one place for discussion and passage of the laws. A republic composed of millions of people, therefore, could not be a true democracy. Democracy, he thought, must either be direct, or nothing; indeed it was only really practicable in very small states or in federations of such states. Large territories, he considered, must either dismember and federalize themselves or abandon the ideal of republican democracy. From the horns of this dilemma there was for him no escape.[34]

33 Frederick II of Prussia, Katherine II of Russia, and Joseph II of Austria were examples of this.

34 Rousseau developed this position in detail in his *Considerations sur le gouvernement de Pologne*. His consistent advocacy of federal republicanism was merely a generalization from the realities of the Swiss regime with which he was most familiar. A republic run by an elected assembly he would have termed ' elective aristocracy.' It played a role of no importance in his theoretical scheme.

The democratic republic as it was eventually to prevail in France was, then, a concept with which the eighteenth century had little familiarity. Notwithstanding this fact three general types of republican outlook made their appearance in the years 1792 to 1796. Each in turn dominated the political scene and was then swept away by the revolutionary whirlwind. Each drew its inspiration from the liberal tradition of the eighteenth century but each emphasized different elements in that common tradition. These types of republicanism corresponded to well defined differences in the social status of the groups adhering to them. We may call them the Girondist, Jacobin and *Sansculotte* types, respectively. They are important because they constituted the three main categories into which French republican theory—as well as republican party organization—has ever since been divided. We will meet these terms many times in the course of our subsequent investigation. Some attempt must accordingly be made here to explain and to justify the meaning which will be attached to them throughout.

Girondist republicanism grew out of the crisis through which the monarchy passed in the summer of 1791 when the king fled to Varennes. Until that time the Assembly had cherished the hope that the throne might be retained as the keystone of the Constitution then being elaborated. But Louis' treason compromised his supporters and caused a split in their ranks. There appeared in the Legislative Assembly a group of men, the *Brissotins*, who insisted that the Crown be jettisoned and a republic be organized. This group was the nucleus of what came to be called the Girondist party. The latter was characterized by the high social status of its adherents and the conservatism of its point of view. The Girondists received their name from the wealthy community which some of them represented. Bordeaux, chief town of the *Gironde,* had made immense progress in maritime commerce during the eighteenth century. It boasted great fortunes acquired from the Antilles trade.[35] Vergniaud, one of the leaders of the Girondist group, was a leading citizen of Bordeaux. He came of wealthy *bourgeois* stock, was a " blue chip " lawyer and a man of luxurious tastes. Brissot, who headed the original republican group formed in the Legislative, was a wealthy humanitarian and a *littérateur*, like Vergniaud a lawyer by profession. Condorcet, who came from the nobility, stood close to the Girondins and was their greatest luminary.

The Girondists adopted a vacillating attitude toward the idea of a republic. In the beginning, as we have just seen, they were in favor of abolishing the monarchy. But the events of August 1792, when an enraged populace thrust the king from the throne and declared for a republic, caused them to change their minds. They feared the pressure of the people of Paris and became convinced that the destruction of the monarchy would be the beginning of further and more violent disorders. Hence they strove to shield the Crown from the people's wrath and to delay as long as possible the trial and sentencing of the king. But with Louis' execution in January 1793 the Girondists shifted their ground again. They saw that a republic could now no longer be avoided and so moved swiftly to elaborate a constitution.

The vacillation of the Girondists on a fundamental matter of state organization was not accidental. They were believers in the inalienable rights of man, and of these they considered that owning, disposing and accumulating property as one saw fit was among the most fundamental. The general welfare, they conceived, could best be promoted by the untrammelled development of private enterprise and wealth. The *form* of the state was to them something quite subordinate to the rights of property and the ideal of *laissez-faire*. Constitutional monarchy or, if need be, republican regime, these were types of government either of which would be acceptable, under certain circumstances, to the commercial interests which they represented.

35 Bordeaux commerce rose in total value from twelve million livres in 1716 to two hundred and fifty in 1782. Sée, *op. cit.*, 332.

These interests would accord their support to a republic provided that it confined itself to the limited political objectives of maintaining order, protecting *bourgeois* property and safeguarding national security.

Condorcet [36] was unwelcome to the Girondists on account of his excessively doctrinaire and abstract opinions, but notwithstanding this fact he clearly expressed many of their characteristic views. He considered that property was sacred. Division of labor ensured a community of interest between individuals and classes which would rule out the need for state intervention in the economic sphere. If clashes of interest should by chance occur, this was due to lack of enlightenment, and might be remedied by more education. Politically Condorcet became in 1791 a convinced republican and was in favor of a one-House Assembly elected by universal suffrage, a principle which he embodied in his draft for a republican constitution in 1793. [37] Condorcet, along with the other Girondists, regarded universal suffrage as a very bold experiment which was necessitated by the conditions prevailing at the time. His constitutional project hence contained provisions designed to impose very real checks upon the will of the democratically elected Assembly. [38]

Thus Girondism resigned itself to the existence of the Republic and embarked upon the experiment cautiously and with reservations. But the period of Girondist ascendancy was brief. In the spring of 1793 the country was in a serious situation. Prices of commodities were rising sharply, there was a bread shortage and the townspeople were getting really hungry. In April Dumouriez deserted to the Austrians and the army was left in confusion. Full scale civil war broke out in La Vendée.

36 For a good summary of Condorcet's life and teachings see J. Salwyn Schapiro, *Condorcet and the Rise of Liberalism* (New York, 1934).

37 Condorcet was a member of the Girondist committee appointed in September 1792 to draw up a constitution for the Republic. The draft submitted in the name of this committee was his work.

38 The rival Girondist and Jacobin projects are ably analyzed and compared by Albert Mathiez in his *Girondins et montagnards* (Paris, 1930).

The situation demanded swift action in defense of the regime, and for this the Girondists with their lukewarm attitude and their unqualified defense of *laissez-faire* were unfitted. The Parisians organized a revolt and drove them from the Assembly. Power passed into the hands of the Jacobins.

In terms of fundamental principle there was little difference to be detected between these two groups, Girondists and Jacobins. Both believed in the sanctity of property rights and both intensely disliked the idea of state intervention in economic life. They were set apart rather by social position and by conflicting ideas with regard to the tactics which must be followed to ensure the triumph of the Revolution. Unlike the Girondists, the Jacobins were not predominantly members of the *haute bourgeoisie* but were of more plebeian, middle-class origin. Robespierre, Danton and St. Just, for example, were all provincial lawyers, professional men of humble birth who had known privation since childhood. Carnot was the son of an obscure notary.[39] From a tactical point of view the Jacobins did not shrink from taking any measure which they considered necessary for winning the war and for defending the Republic from its enemies both within and without. The Girondists, good *bourgeois* that they were, had stood for the abolition of seignorial forms of property and privilege, but they had shrunk from taking the harsh measures that were needed to accomplish this end under wartime conditions. The Girondists had been lukewarm about the prosecution of the war, and the Jacobins could claim, not without justice, that the long series of defeats which followed the victories of 1792 were due to Girondist treason and incompetence.[40] The Jacobins, on the other hand, pressed for the energetic organization of the national defense

39 The Jacobins also recruited to their banner a number of *déclassés*, like Jean-Paul Marat and Anacharsis Cloots.

40 After August 10, 1792, according to Michelet, the Girondist party became " ... the asylum of royalism, the protective mask under which reaction could remain in Paris in the presence of the Revolution." Quoted by Mathiez, *Girondins et montagnards, op. cit.*, 13.

as the only way to save the Revolution; and they wished to take whatever measures were necessary to destroy finally the power of the feudal aristocracy, to curb the influence of the priests—most of whom had aristocratic or Girondist sympathies —and to attach the masses to loyal support of the new state.

The Jacobins, like everyone else, had been strongly royalist at the outset of the Revolution. When, however, it became clear that an end must be made of the monarchy, they committed themselves irrevocably to the organization of a republic. In the teeth of Girondist opposition they tried the king, executed him, and embarked on open warfare with the royalists. They established a war dictatorship in the name of republican democracy. They held, further, certain theories concerning state intervention which fitted them, far more than the consistent disciples of *laissez-faire*, to carry out the radical measures necessary to ensure the success of the Revolution. They, and preeminently Robespierre, insisted that on given occasions and for given ends, public interest could override the rights of individual property owners. This conception was derived primarily from Rousseau; if, as the latter held, the people were sovereign, and empowered to make such laws as they chose for the common good, then clearly they might see fit at times to limit such natural prerogatives as the right to the enjoyment of property or to freedom of speech for the general good. The Jacobins, it might be concluded, were a party of the middle class with a more clear-sighted view than the Girondists of the measures necessary for the success of the Revolution during the years of foreign and civil war.

The Jacobins justified the intervention of the state mainly as a war emergency with the sole objective of defending the political regime. This position brought them into conflict with the spokesmen of the extreme Left who demanded state intervention as an economic weapon and as an instrument of social justice. As the Revolution progressed and the distress of the mass of the people increased, new champions arose to contest with the Jacobins the monopoly of leadership and to press for measures to mitigate the economic crisis and to redistribute the land.[41]

These popular representatives were for the most part artisans or priests.[42] Their origin was reflected in the epithet *Sansculotte*, a term which denoted those who did not wear the breeches which were the badge of the well-to-do. By a natural progression it was applied to and came to denote those who defended any fundamental redistribution of wealth in the interests of the poor. During the Revolution various *Sansculotte* proposals were put forward for which their authors usually paid the penalty on the guillotine.[43] But the first systematic formulation of the *Sansculotte* ideal was produced by François-Noel Babeuf in 1795. Babeuf, it must be emphasized, was himself the leader of an important republican faction, the *Conspiration des Égaux*. He believed that a true republic, based upon social equality, could only be introduced by the overthrow of the *bourgeois* regime at the hands of an organized, conspiratorial minority and with the aid of force. Babeuf was vague as to the means by which true social equality could be maintained; but, like Meslier and Morelly before him, he stood for the abolition of individual rights in landed property and for the institution of some system of common ownership of national wealth. He was certain that no republic, however democratic it was in political organization,

41 Seignorial dues were abolished in principle in 1789, but the peasantry found that in practice they were obliged to redeem them in cash under burdensome conditions. The early revolutionary assemblies, further, did little to satisfy the peasants' land hunger, Church estates being put up for sale in lots which for the most part only a man of means could afford to buy.

42 Gaspard Chaumette, a famous member of the *Commune*, was the son of a jeweller or cobbler (it is not clear which). Antoine Momoro, his associate, was a master-printer. Jacques Hébert, one of the most articulate of all popular spokesmen, was the son of an Alençon goldsmith. Jacques Roux, that violent and grandiose revolutionary figure, was a parish priest of the same unpolished type as Jean Meslier himself.

43 Roux, Hébert, Momoro and Chaumette were all guillotined during the first months of 1794.

could be considered adequate so long as wide differences in wealth and status existed among its members.[44]

Such were the three types of republican outlook that appeared at the time of the Great Revolution, in the years from 1792 to 1796. Each summed up and carried forward the liberal tradition of the Enlightenment but each stressed different elements in that tradition. During the nineteenth century *Sansculotte* republicanism produced social theories that more or less deeply affected the other types of republican thought, but it had not by 1914 given rise to any one doctrine that was practically and theoretically dominant in the French state. But the Girondist and Jacobin traditions had been taken up and elaborated into what were to become successively the dominant philosophies of the Third Republic during the period 1870 to 1914. With these traditions and the ideas that grew out of them the following essay will be mainly concerned.

IV

The time of republican triumph during the Great Revolution was brief. The First Republic drew its strength from the conditions created by the war crisis of 1792. But by 1794 the very successes of revolutionary arms led to a weakening of the regime. Republican victories produced a reaction on the part of the wealthy classes against the war dictatorship and its unwelcome controls. A united war effort degenerated into a series of inner political conflicts and the country thus weakened became an easy prey to a demagogue's ambition. Napoleon's *coup d'état* of 1799 inaugurated an era of nearly three-quarters of a century during which royal dynasties ruled France with only brief interruptions. The narrow mercantile and landed oligarchy who benefited from this period of more or less autocratic rule were strangers to the liberal traditions of popular sovereignty, the lay state and civil rights. At times it seemed

---

[44] Babeuf was put on trial for his conspiratorial activities and guillotined in 1797.

as though the very memory of the early republican experiment had all but died out.

The governments of the dynastic era, as we may call it, were either frankly dictatorial, as in the case of Napoleon III, or, as in the case of the Bourbon and Orleanist regimes, they conceded the franchise and some measure of parliamentary rule to the wealthy landed and mercantile interests. But the course of events showed that the stability of a "property owners' state" could not for long be maintained in nineteenth century France. Royalism during this period discredited itself in the eyes of the mass of the people and thus made inevitable the approach of a time when republicanism would be recognized as the sole guardian and transmitter of the revolutionary traditions inherited from the eighteenth century.

Industrialization, in the first place, broke up the comparative stability of the existing order. France, it is true, lagged behind England and Belgium in the development of machinery and in the application of power to industrial processes; but the tempo of her economic change became increasingly rapid as the century advanced.[45] In the very first years of the century, under the Napoleonic regime, there were unmistakable signs that a new era was at hand;[46] in the period of Napoleon III's rule, from 1852 to 1870, the factory system gradually achieved predominance in most of the leading branches of national industry.[47] The old order of society and its ideas of autocratic government, already weakened by the revolutionary movement let loose in 1789, began to crumble with the advent of the machine.

45 "France," J. H. Clapham wisely wrote, "never went through an industrial revolution. There was a gradual transformation, a slow shifting of her economic centre of gravity from the side of agriculture to that of industry, and a slow change in the methods of industrial organization." *The Economic Development of France and Germany, 1815-1914* (Cambridge, 3rd ed., 1928), 53.

46 Sée, *Ésquisse, op. cit.*, 411, and Germain Martin, *Histoire économique et financière* (Paris, 1927), 343.

47 Sée, *ibid.*, 461, and Clapham, *op. cit.*, chapter 10, *passim*.

Industrialism, in the second place, brought about a gradual change in the class structure. There arose in France a group of business men, of industrial capitalists, whose interests conflicted at many points with the magnates of commerce who were the effective rulers of the country during the dynastic era. These elements, not in themselves very numerous, at least at the beginning of the nineteenth century, were made redoubtable to the existing political order by the support which on occasion they received from the propertyless masses. Indeed, perhaps the most significant of all the consequences of industrialization was the concentration in the towns of a proletarian Fourth Estate.[48] The masses, disfranchised and deprived of any political power, existed under cruel conditions of life which the most militant among them searched for means to change. Throughout the nineteenth century these workers were first to last the most consistent, energetic and heroic fighters for the republic. More than once during the dynastic era they came out onto the streets at the appeal of *bourgeois* republican leaders and overthrew the existing regime. Discerning observers early realized that no system of government could be considered solidly established in France that continued to deny power to these new classes that were being greatly extended by the industrial revolution.

48 The concentration of industry that was a direct product of the advent of the machine age brought with it an enormous increase of population in the urban centers. The rural population, stationary since the middle of the century, began to decline absolutely after 1876. The urban population, on the other hand, began to increase rapidly in the earliest years of Louis Philippe's reign. In the decade 1836 to 1846, for example, the population of Roubaix increased from 8 000 to 34,000 souls and that of St. Étienne from 16,000 to 54,000. The total population increased from 36,000,000 in 1856 to 38,000,000 in 1866. The events of 1870 to 1871 brought a temporary decline, but the peak of 1866 had been passed two decades later, despite the loss of Alsace. This secular net increase of population may be considered a significant reflection of the development of industrialization. These figures are taken from *Statistique générale de la France. Resultats statistiques du denombrement de 1891* (Paris, 1894), 32, 65; *Annuaire statistique* (" Résumé retrospectif. État et mouvement de la population.") ; and Sée, *op. cit.*, 435.

These factors were to ensure the eventual success of the republican movement, but after 1800 it went through a long winter of repression and persecution.[49] Save during the brief interlude of the Second Republic it was compelled to conduct its activities for the most part in secret. Doctrinally republicanism remained during the dynastic era in an amorphous condition. Girondist, Jacobin and *Sansculotte* tendencies all had their own leaders, newspapers and party organizations. They carried on heated political struggles and controversies among themselves. But of notable contributions to republican theory there were few.[50] In this period thinkers were preoccupied as much with the new problems raised by the advent of an industrial age as with the narrower questions of political theory. They strove to analyze and to explain the changes occurring in society and to put forward solutions for the evils of life in a capitalist world. Thus the social thought of the dynastic era was enriched by the contributions of Henri de St. Simon and Auguste Comte, of Pierre-Joseph Proudhon and Louis Blanc, of Auguste Blanqui and Pierre Leroux, to name but the most outstanding. As will become clear in the sequel the work of these men was to modify and deepen the channels along which republican thought had traditionally run. But at the time the relationship of their analyses to traditional ideals and tactics was far from clear. Republican doctrine needed time to assimilate the materials that a new age had presented to it.[51]

49 The standard history of the republican party during the dynastic era is Georges Weill, *Histoire du parti républicain en France, 1814-1870* (Paris, *nouvelle édition*, 1928). For republican doctrine during this period see I. Tchernoff, *Le Parti républicain sous la monarchie de juillet: formation et évolution de la doctrine républicaine* (Paris, 1901), and *Le Parti républicain au coup d'état et sous le Second Empire* (Paris, 1906).

50 The most famous republican writers of the dynastic era, Jules Michelet, Alexis de Tocqueville and Edgar Quinet were all historians rather than political theorists.

51 " The intrusion of socialism, which found itself ill at ease within the framework of the old political order, was to put everything in question again and to require a new effort of assimilation and adaptation ... " Tchernoff, *Le Parti républicain sous la monarchie de juillet, op. cit.*, 262.

By the end of the nineteenth century there had emerged from the Girondist and Jacobin traditions mature and clearly formulated bodies of republican philosophy. These possessed that unity, coherence and system which themselves constitute a source of strength in organizing people, in clarifying their thought and in directing their political struggles. They had assimilated many of the new ideas produced by previous social thinkers and had become closely connected with legal political parties. Each in turn occupied, in the period from 1870 to 1914, a dominating and almost official position as philosophies of the republican state. These two schools I have termed neo-Girondist and neo-Jacobin because their affiliation with the Girondist and Jacobin traditions of the first Republic is apparent even though each had achieved a synthesis uniquely applicable to the conditions that prevailed in France in the later nineteenth century. The *Sansculotte* tradition during this same period was largely taken over by Marxist theory, and assumed the form of socialism. Assuming a new form it continued to be a vital force in republican thought, but unlike the other schools it did not become politically dominant during the period nor did it eventuate in a single coherent body of doctrine. As will be seen, the *Sansculotte* tradition exerted a considerable influence upon the other types of republican thought, but it failed to supplant them. For this reason it has seemed well to exclude socialist republicanism from direct consideration in the present study and to concentrate our attention upon the neo-Jacobin and neo-Girondist schools.

PART I

REPUBLICAN THEORIES OF THE NINETEENTH
CENTURY GIRONDE

INTRODUCTORY

FOR the first three quarters of the nineteenth century France was ruled by a royalist oligarchy whose fortunes were based mainly on land, commerce and banking. This wealthy section of the *bourgeoisie* adapted itself fairly easily to successive dynasties; it remained throughout this period the most influential, and in fact the dominating group, in French society.[1] The leaders of this oligarchy were men like Adolphe Thiers, François Guizot, and Victor de Broglie. They were by preference Orleanist, but they made shift to adapt themselves to the conditions of Louis Napoleon's Bonapartist regime and later to those prevailing under the Third Republic.

By the end of the third quarter of the century the domination of this oligarchy was drawing to a close. The growth of industrialism was bringing forward a new element in the *bourgeoisie* that was strongly disposed to contest the Orleanists' monopoly of state power. It had generated pressure for the political enfranchisement of the masses which no political party dared any longer ignore.

Under these conditions the appearance of a liberal republican party was eminently logical. The liberal republicans became organized in the late 1860's and rose to power under the meteoric leadership of Léon Gambetta. Thrusting aside the dynasts they became, after the elections of 1876, the dominant political party in France. They retained this leadership until nearly the end of the century.

The conditions for the appearance of the liberal republican party were created by the collapse of the Bonapartist Empire and by the Franco-Prussian war. The effect of the *débâcle* of 1870 and 1871 was to discredit the dynastic *bourgeoisie*. During the Empire the latter had, as it were, sheltered behind the dictator. His fall brought them face to face with the masses

1 The term *dynastic bourgeoisie* may fittingly be applied to this group to denote a middle-class oligarchy with a strong preference for royalist as opposed to republican regimes.

when general elections were held in January 1871, and when the Bordeaux Assembly came into being.

The Bordeaux Assembly, composed mainly of Orleanists and Legitimists, was dominated by Thiers. Thiers was in favor of the conclusion of unconditional peace with Germany at the earliest possible moment. He was squarely opposed by the republicans who, throughout the country but above all in Paris, were for a continuation of the war against the invading Prussian.

Compromise with Paris was something that never entered the calculations of Thiers and the Assembly. They moved swiftly to smash the capital's opposition, and achieved their end in the greatest of all nineteenth century French civil wars. By the suppression of the *Commune* and the pitiless slaughter and exile of its supporters, Thiers and his cohorts earned for themselves the contempt and the hatred of the mass of the people.

The Paris *Commune* constituted a landmark in French history, and its effects upon French politics were felt for many years. The immediate result of this cataclysm was to smash the political power of the French working class and of the republican forces in general.

In the years following the *Commune,* from 1871 to 1875, the Assembly attempted desperately to revive dynastic rule; but it was hampered both by its own internal divisions and by its general unpopularity throughout the country. Notwithstanding the reign of terror which they practised against the republicans, the dynasts were compelled to give way to the growing republican movement. They were compelled, against their will, to formulate a constitution for the Republic and to arrange for the general elections which signed their own political death warrant. In 1876 a republican majority was returned to Parliament.

The liberal republicans were swept into power by these elections. They dominated the French political scene for the next twenty years, and became known, toward the end of the 1870's, as 'opportunists.' [2] This label was given them for their failure to realize and carry out the radical democratic program with which they had gone to the electorate in 1876.[3] The reason for the procrastinating behavior of the liberal republicans is not far to seek: in achieving state power they found themselves essentially in a contradictory situation. On the one hand, their political interests required that they should consolidate the Republic, make war against the Church and the royalist factions that were intringuing for their downfall, and drive the reactionaries out of the key public positions which they monopolized. On the other hand, fear of the republican Left, that is, of the Jacobins and *Sansculottes*, whose revival was menacing their political position, dictated that the liberal republicans make peace with their erstwhile enemies, come to terms with the Church, and in general rely upon the conservative forces in society to impede the advance of radicalism.[4]

It is in terms of this dilemma that the contradictory and half-way measures taken by the opportunists to consolidate and establish the Republic may be explained. The Second Chamber, for example, that had been set up by the Constitution of 1875, remained for many years a stronghold of Orleanism; but the opportunists carefully refrained from attacking it or attempting its abolition. The Church, again, financed by state funds and possessing its own school system, was the single most important support of French royalism, and a source of anti-republican propaganda and intrigue. The opportunists denounced this situation, but did little to change it; on the contrary, they refrained from abrogating the *Concordat* of 1801 which regulated the relationship of Church and state, and

2 The term was first coined by the journalist Rochefort in an editorial of 1879 in *Les Droits de l'homme* entitled "*Les opportunistes.*" As used by him it signified the postponement, i. e., abandonment, of necessary reforms.

3 This program was based upon a mandate presented by the electors of Belleville to their candidate Gambetta in 1869. It included separation of Church and state, freedom of press and meeting, free and compulsory elementary education and freedom of unionization for the working-class.

4 For a further definition of radicalism, see below, 120.

thus refused to deprive Catholicism of official sanction and financial support.

The term 'opportunist' carries the implication that the liberal republicans operated empirically, that they possessed no political philosophy or set of political principles. Such was not the case. Liberal republican theory in many ways reflected the contradictions of the opportunist position; but between the years 1870 and 1890 this theory was formulated into a comprehensive and systematic body of doctrine. The latter bore a direct relationship to the Girondist thought of the Great Revolution, but was also adapted to the problems and conditions of the industrial age. Liberal republican thought may, therefore, be termed *neo-Girondist*. This term characterizes the nature and derivation of the doctrine as well as the social and class position of its supporters.

Neo-Girondist political philosophy was elaborated by two of France's most eminent liberal thinkers, Charles Renouvier and Émile Littré. Their work expounded the fundamental principles and objectives of the dominant political trend of the last quarter of the nineteenth century; and it is of significance both as the classic formulation of this trend and for its subsequent influence upon the thought of the radical republicans, or neo-Jacobins.

The leading theoretical contentions of these two thinkers were in many important respects similar. They believed that the *bourgeoisie* as a whole, and not merely one exclusive and influential section of that class, should rule France. They believed that the *form* through which this rule should be exercized was the Republic, and that the political basis of this rule—as opposed to the constitutional, economic, or legal basis—should lie in the institution of universal suffrage. Their philosophy was characterized by antagonism to the Church and to royalism on the one hand, and to what they termed 'Jacobinism' on the other.[5] Economically their doctrine was characterized by a

5 'Jacobinism' to the liberal republicans signified all the popular forces opposed to them, whether they were Jacobin or *Sansculotte*. They identified Jacobinism with popular movements, anarchy, public disturbance, etc. See below, 62, 65.

rigid adherence to *laissez-faire*, and by an insistence that working class organization, whether through trade unions or co-operative, could solve the main problems confronting the French proletariat without recourse to revolutionary strategy.

Littré and Renouvier's philosophical assumptions were in many ways opposed, and they founded distinct and even antagonistic schools of thought: Renouvier was a neo-Kantian, to whom the only kind of progress in the world was the moral advance, the degree of rationality, which might be achieved by successive generations of men. Littré, on the other hand, was a follower of Auguste Comte, strongly influenced by a determinist conception of history that taught that progress was in some sense automatic, and beyond the control of human struggle and volition. To Renouvier, again, the Republic was an ideal, to be striven for and defended on principle; to Comte it was a ' sociological experiment,' an empirical, *ad hoc* solution to the question of state organization.

The practical contradiction between these two schools of thought was more apparent than real. Littré, toward the end of his life, abandoned the Comtian thesis of the inevitability of progress; after 1869 he approximated increasingly to Renouvier's position on this point. Yet the differences between the two schools must not be minimized. They resulted in significant differences in the influence of the two bodies of doctrine. Littré's subsequent theoretical importance was small, but the sociological methods of analysis which he had used were taken up and developed by later republican thinkers. Renouvier's influence was great; his formulation of neo-Girondism has been a major source of French liberal thinking ever since. In general, neo-Girondist thought has carried on the liberal, anticlerical traditions of the Enlightenment and of the early Revolution: this connection is of the clearest and most demonstrable kind. Renouvier's writings, in addition, were consciously inspired by the individualist, anti-Catholic traditions of the French Reformation.

CHAPTER I

CHARLES RENOUVIER AND THE PHILOSOPHIC LIBERALS

I

Renouvier [1] was born at Montpellier in 1815 into a family of the well-to-do and enlightened *bourgeoisie*. He had an eager, speculative mind not at all suited to the *dilettante* life which the family fortune enabled him to lead; [2] consequently he became attracted to the study of philosophy, and in 1839 took part in an essay competition promoted by the Academy of Moral and Political Science on the Cartesian system and its place in the history of philosophical thought. Unlike Jean-Jacques Rousseau in a somewhat similar situation, Renouvier did not win, but his career was settled. Starting with the publication of a philosophical text in 1842 [3] Renouvier embarked upon a lifetime of creative writing on social questions that was to end only a few years before his death in 1903. [4]

Renouvier was not merely a cabinet philosopher; throughout his life he retained the characteristics which he manifested early in his youth as a *bourgeois* revolutionary with passionate republican convictions and a bitter hatred of all types of dynastic government. In 1843 he attached himself to *La Nouvelle*

1 The following biographical details are borrowed mainly from Louis Foucher, *La Jeunesse de Renouvier et sa première philosophie 1815-1854* (Paris, 1927), and from François Pillon, "Nécrologie: Charles Renouvier," *Année philosophique*, XIV (1903), 309-311.

2 Mme. Juliette Adam professed to a great admiration for Renouvier, describing him as "a man of noble and searching intellect, with a thirst for knowledge...." *Mes premières années littéraires et politiques* (Paris, 1904), 33.

3 *Manuel de philosophie moderne* (Paris, 1842).

4 The last years of Renouvier's life were given over principally to the elaboration of his religious ideas. A complete listing of all his writings will be found in Louis Foucher's excellent *Bibliographie chronologique de Charles Renouvier—Thèse complémentaire* (Paris, 1927).

Encyclopédie; inaugurated in 1836 by the philosophers Renaud and Leroux for the purpose of spreading St. Simonian ideas, this project grouped a number of what might be termed republican encyclopedists, the most eminent of whom were Frédéric Le Play and Geoffroy St. Hilaire.[5] When Louis Philippe was overthrown in February 1848 the encyclopedists, somewhat to their surprise, found themselves in control of the educational affairs of the Second Republic; Hippolyte Carnot, one of their number, was appointed Minister of Public Instruction. Renouvier became a member of a legislative committee whose function it was to draft a law that would provide for free, compulsory, universal, and non-sectarian elementary education.

This term of office came to an abrupt close after the June days.[6] Renouvier, at the instance of Carnot, had written a manual for the purpose of promoting republican propaganda among the people.[7] The royalists in the National Assembly seized upon this work with the charge that it was socialist and egalitarian—which indeed it was—and used it as a pretext to upset Carnot and wreck his education bill. Renouvier's connection with the Ministry of Public Instruction was severed, and his manual was confiscated and burned. Enraged both at his own treatment and at the horrors of the June massacre, Renouvier retorted with a second edition in which he castigated the Republic for the blood that it had spilled. He joined

5 Renouvier contributed philosophical articles to the Encyclopedia until it ceased its somewhat erratic publication in 1847.

6 The June days, 1848, is a term denoting the civil war that broke out at that time between liberal and *sansculotte* republicans. Fought ostensibly over the issue of labor's role in the revolutionary government and the future of the public works project then in operation, this conflict was due fundamentally to the moderates' desire to rid themselves of their embarrassing proletarian rival. The net result of the war was to weaken all the republican parties and hence to pave the way for the resurrection of Bonapartist dictatorship.

7 *Manuel républicain de l'homme et du citoyen*, edited by J. Thomas (Paris, 1904).

the opposition and devoted himself thenceforth to journalism, serving on the editorial board of *La Presse populaire,* a Jacobin organ, and contributing to *Liberté de penser,* a university magazine with strong democratic tendencies.[8]

In 1851 Louis Napoleon's *coup d'état* marked the return of France to dictatorship. Renouvier went into retirement and during the long years of the Napoleonic regime gave himself over exclusively to philosophical pursuits. His mature thought dates from the publication of the *Critical Essays* in this period,[9] and from the *Science of Morals* which followed shortly after.[10] These works not only established Renouvier's reputation as a thinker,[11] but laid the philosophical basis for the neo-Girondist republican writings of succeeding years.

When the Second Empire collapsed Renouvier was ready to resume his activities as an educator and mentor of the republican party. In 1872, in collaboration with François Pillon,[12] he began publication of *La Critique philosophique.* This review, appearing bi-monthly and later monthly for seventeen consecutive years,[13] had, at one time or another, many

8 *Liberté de penser* was founded in 1847 by the deists Jacques Amedée and Jules Simon, and became almost at once republican. Strongly anticlerical, it demanded the separation of Church and state and advocated elementary lay education as an indispensable condition for the establishment of a republican regime. See Georges Weill, *Histoire de l'idée laique en France au 19ᵉ siècle* (Paris, 1929), 106-113.

9 *Essais de critique générale* (Paris, 1854-1864).

10 *Science de la morale* (Paris, 1869).

11 Renouvier first became widely known in 1868, when Félix Ravaisson-Mollien's *La Philosophie en France au 19ᵉ siècle* first drew the attention of the philosophic world to the importance of his *Critical Essays.*

12 Republican philosopher, critic, and journalist (1830-1914). Pillon's qualities as a writer admirably supplemented those of Renouvier. Doctrinally they appear to have been in almost perfect agreement. Pillon's collaboration with Renouvier lasted for about a quarter of a century in a remarkably sustained identity of aims and interests.

13 Renouvier and Pillon had cooperated in the production of the organ *Année philosophique* in 1867, but the events of 1870-1871 put an end to this venture. *Philosophical Criticism* was thus a continuation of the previous

eminent collaborators. But the bulk of its contributions, both articles, shorter notices, and book reviews, came from the pens of the editors themselves. *La Critique philosophique* was published over a period (1872-1889) roughly coincidental with the predominance of the liberal republicans, or opportunists, in French political life. This work was addressed to the republican party headed by Gambetta, and offered it all the elements of a consistent doctrine. In the pages of this journal the leading ideas of neo-Girondism were set forth. Here liberal republicanism received classical expression; here, too, its weaknesses as a body of theory, the problems and inconsistencies that beset it, were profoundly and excellently mirrored.

II

Renouvier's political theory in its maturity continued the Girondist traditions of the eighteenth century and developed them to meet the special problems raised by the coming of the industrial age. This fact, central to a correct understanding of nineteenth century liberal republicanism, may be illustrated by reference to the influences which played a major part in the shaping of Renouvier's thought.

Renouvier was, above all else, a child of the Enlightenment. His father possessed a magnificent library of the eighteenth century classics; and here Renouvier in his youth had browsed for hours at a time. His creed derived much from Voltaire's humanitarianism, Rousseau's natural religion and Condorcet's faith in human nature and human perfectibility. These antecedents and these intellectual traditions Renouvier constantly and proudly acknowledged; he evidently accepted them with little reserve. The concepts of natural rights and the sanctity of the individual found in him a worthy continuator.

An Enlightenment influence of particular importance for Renouvier's thought was the work of Immanuel Kant. To the latter he owed a twofold debt for his phenomenalist approach

journal, but on broader lines. Pillon resumed publication of the *Année philosophique* in 1890 and continued it until his death.

to social studies and for his conception of human psychology. The French philosophers of the Enlightenment had shown faith in the power of reason to solve human problems without feeling the need to attempt a critical appraisal of the nature of reason itself. This task was left to Kant, who explored the relationship of human cognition to the material world on the one side and to the invisible world of morals and religion on the other. Stung by the sceptical taunts of David Hume, he subjected the concept of reason to an extraordinarily thorough and critical analysis. But Kantian doctrines, and in particular the method which Kant used in arriving at them, received almost no attention in France during the first half of the nineteenth century.[14] Renouvier was among the first French philosophers to be profoundly influenced by him, and, with certain modifications, adopted and expounded Kant's ideas under the title of 'criticism.'

'Criticism' may be summarized as an attempt to reconcile determinism in the world of matter with the concept of human freedom and morality. It taught that there existed a real, phenomenal world, bound together according to natural laws, by necessary connections, such as cause and effect. But man, this doctrine continued, must be understood as a rational, self-determining being who stood *outside* the phenomenal sequence in respect to his moral decisions and moral freedom. By virtue of the latter man could change and influence the course of events in the real world. Hence the possibility of man's mastery over nature, of progress, was predicted; conditioned, however, by moral progress, by man's mastery over himself and his own actions.

The term criticism was applied by Renouvier not merely to these Kantian conclusions, or central elements of Kant's doc-

14 George Boas, *French Philosophies of the Romantic Period* (Baltimore, 1925), 172, 183. During this period the empiricist psychology of Condillac was predominant in the schools. The empiricists, it must be pointed out, did not subject the faculty of reason to a critical examination, but reduced it to a mere psychological "attention" to sense-data.

trine; it was applied also to the *method* employed in establishing this position. 'Criticism' as used both by Kant himself and his disciples denoted the preparatory investigations necessary for the refutation of Hume, for the analysis of reason and of the nature of the world. This, in its turn, involved the evaluation of much historical material, and was inevitably accompanied by historical research.

The conception of man as a being endowed with sovereign reason, free to change the world, to decide between good and evil, was not in itself a religious one; but historically it had religious roots. The Protestant reformation everywhere in the sixteenth century raised its banner over the issue of the individual as the sole arbiter of his acts, his faith and his moral destiny. Renouvier was by temperament inclined to a mystical religiosity, and held throughout his life deistic beliefs that were entirely compatible with Kantian criticism [15] and afforded one more similarity between his position and that of the *philosophes*. Like them, too—and like Voltaire in particular—he combined deeply religious beliefs about the universe with anticlericalism. All his life he fought against the Catholic Church with as deep a hatred and as mordant a pen as any of his sixteenth or eighteenth century predecessors; and the inspiration for this battle he drew, as we shall see, directly from both these sources.

Man as an active agent in a world governed by ascertainable law, investigating and analysing that world according to rational method that repudiated authoritarianism and superstition without negating a religious attitude toward life and morality, such, in a sentence, was Renouvier's conception of 'criticism.' One writer has aptly summarized this approach as a system " at once idealistic and phenomenalist, which un-

15 Kant's argument for the existence of God rejected the traditional theological demonstrations and consisted in *deducing* that existence from the reality of man's moral experience. *Kritik der reinen Vernunft*, 2nd edition: English edition, translated by J. M. D. Meiklejohn in the Everyman series (London, 1934), 346-367, 462, 469.

dertakes to establish, as conclusions of critical study, man's liberty and personality, an order of nature compatible with contingency, and the existence of an author of the universe. . . ." [16]

The ideas of the Enlightenment had been set forth in the main to combat the *ancien régime,* to list the grievances of the *bourgeoisie,* and to expound the latter's interests with regard to the safeguarding of property and of civic rights. The Girondists had been the first, during the Great Revolution, to combine the liberal ideas of the *philosophes* with the advocacy of a republican regime based upon universal suffrage. This precedent of liberal republicanism in the eighteenth century was a very important one for the neo-Girondists, and in particular for Renouvier and the liberal republicans of the 1870's; and this point will become abundantly clear in the sequel. But, valuable as the Girondist tradition was, its creed had been a narrowly political one; it could not survive as a dominant expression of the liberal republican movement, much less win mass support, without sufficient modification to meet the changed conditions of French society.

In achieving this development of Girondist thought and in producing the manifestations of Renouvier's neo-Girondism, the influence of early nineteenth century socialism was of central importance. The chief factor underlying the evolution of Girondism was the growth of industrialism with its revolutionary implications for the economic structure and for political institutions. Renouvier while still a very young man was fully aware of the great changes occurring in society. In the early thirties he had come under the influence of St. Simon, whose keen mind had foreseen the advent of an industrial age and the necessity for a social revolution in the interests of the industrial classes. He had collaborated, as we have seen, with

16 Lucien Lévy-Bruhl, *History of Modern Philosophy in France* (Chicago, 1924), 449, 450. For a discussion of criticism see also Theodore Merz, *History of European Thought in the 19th Century* (Edinburgh, 1896-1914), III, 48 ff.

the Christian Socialist Pierre Leroux, to whom a republic and a St. Simonian socialist order were synonymous as a means of emancipating the working-class. But the problem did not present itself to Renouvier as one of the abolition of private property; his concern, rather, was to reconcile the traditional Girondist conception of the sanctity of *bourgeois* property with the conflicts of the new industrial age and the challenge of a new, propertyless class.

The thinker who most influenced him in arriving at a solution was Charles Fourier; Fourier conceived of man as a social being actuated by strong feelings that bound him to his fellow men by bonds of what he termed 'social solidarity.' These arose from the fact that men undertook common action for common purposes; and this associationist concept early became and always remained fundamental to neo-Girondist thought.[17] Practically—and this was an important implication —it involved recognition of the desirability of working-class association, both in the form of cooperatives and trade-unions, as a means toward the 'emancipation' of the proletariat.[18] But it is to be noted that emancipation here had a special meaning; it was used to denote the process by which proletarians, acquiring capital through cooperative action, and becoming self-employing, *would thus cease to be proletarian.* To the neo-Girondists Fourierist influence was expressed in the form of a panacea that would *abolish* the propertyless class and would hence resolve class conflict simply by removing the

17 " Renouvier," wrote Richard, " had belonged in his youth to the associationist school of Charles Fourier. He never broke with it and always took account of its judgment. The *Critique philosophique* . . . included Fourierist collaborators, notably Charles Pellarin." Gaston Richard, *La Question sociale et le mouvement philosophique au 19ᵉ siècle* (Paris, 1914), 276.

18 Fourier held that association should be voluntary; Louis Blanc later contributed the idea that cooperatives should be aided and encouraged by the state. On the significance of associationism as a basis of neo-Girondist philosophy, see below, 70.

workers as the chief threat to the stability of the *bourgeois* Republic.[19]

Renouvier combined these various influences into a theory that expressed in a systematic way the outlook of French liberal republicanism in the last quarter of the nineteenth century. Some attention must now be given to an examination of the leading elements in this doctrine.

III

Renouvier's political philosophy [20] was founded upon the belief that the republican state was the highest point, either in the ancient or the modern world, which men had achieved in their historic struggle for emancipation. It was in itself, he considered, a condition for further human progress. Renouvier thought of republicanism as the culmination of an age-long battle against tyranny and superstition. After the manner of Condorcet and the *philosophes,* he viewed history [21] as an ef-

19 The French working-class believed in the associationist ideal until the Marxists demonstrated in the 1880's its complete inadequacy as a serious program for the emancipation of the proletariat.

20 The single most useful work on Renouvier's political and social thought is Roger Picard, *La Philosophie sociale de Renouvier* (Paris, 1908), though this is in many ways outdated. A synopsis of Renouvier's philosophy in relation to his republican ideas is provided by O. Hamelin, *Le Système de Renouvier* (Paris, 1927). P. Mouy, *L'Idée de progrès dans la philosophie de Renouvier* (Paris, 1927) ; Foucher, *La Jeunesse de Renouvier et sa première philosophie, op. cit.,* and Irène Cornwell, *Les Principes du droit dans la philosophie de Charles Renouvier. Le droit international* (Paris, c. 1922), all deal with special aspects of Renouvier's republicanism. A brief estimate of the philosopher's work and influence is contained in the obituary appearing in the *Revue de métaphysique et morale,* XI (1903), *supplément:* Séptembre, 1, and in Louis Prat, *Charles Renouvier, philosophe, sa doctrine, sa vie* (Pamiers, 1937). Commentary in English is both poor and scant. See in particular Roger Soltau, *French Political Thought in the 19th Century, op. cit.,* 306-321 ; Daniel Parodi, " Renouvier," in the *Encyclopedia of the Social Sciences* (New York, 1934), XIII, 288-289; and John A. Scott, "Main Themes of Republican Thought during the Formative Years of the Third French Republic " (Columbia University Master's Essay, 1946), 32-43.

21 Renouvier's principal historical works are: *Introduction à la philosophie analytique de l'histoire* (Paris, 1864) ; *Uchronie* (Paris, 1876) ; and *Philo-*

fort to shake off the physical, moral and intellectual domination of kings and priests. The outcome of this process, which
was in no way foreordained or inevitable, but subject to re-
versals and defeats, was the establishment, at the time and
place of furthest advance, of democratic republics.

In holding this position Renouvier was of course doing little
more than generalize from the leading events of modern French
history. In the last quarter of the nineteenth century, as a
result of hundreds of years of struggle against the old order,
a liberal-democratic Republic had at last been instituted with
a fair chance of survival. This liberal Republic based upon
universal suffrage, along with its predecessors of 1792 and
1848, Renouvier regarded as the *ne plus ultra* of human progress up to his own day.

Renouvier saw only too clearly that the success of the Republic was contingent upon continued struggle against the
forces of the Right that sought to overthrow it; the time was
by no means over when it might be necessary once more to
make a revolution against royalism or dictatorship.[22] But this
very fact raised a problem with regard to the right to revolution. It appeared incontestable to Renouvier that at certain
times insurrection was necessary and justified; it was only by
revolutionary, popular action that the Republic had triumphed
in 1792 and in 1848. In 1852, again, it had become clear that
revolution would once more be necessary to set aside the
tyranny of Napoleon III. Similarly, in the early years of the
Third Republic the opportunists had only a very precarious
hold upon the state, and it was impossible to predict that an

---

sophie analytique de l'histoire (Paris, 1896-1898). *La Critique philosophique*
abounds in historical essays.

22 Renouvier, in direct contrast to Auguste Comte, never failed to stress
that social progress was the result of human struggle, and that it was in no
way foreordained or inevitable. Lucien Lévy-Bruhl, writing in 1899, pointed
out that the focus of Renouvier's philosophy was action, and that it was this
that had contributed chiefly to establish its influence among contemporaries.
History of Modern Philosophy, op. cit., 450, 451.

appeal would not once more have to be made to the people to overthrow an usurping royalist or Bonapartist regime.

At the same time the liberal republicans found themselves in sharp opposition to the Left. The latter, as we have already noted, was not by any means a homogeneous force and contained both Jacobin and *Sansculotte* elements which were sharply divided among themselves. But the neo-Girondists bothered little with this detail. All republican forces that were hostile to their tradition they designated as Jacobin. They used this term—quite incorrectly as it happens—to denote all doctrines that, in the century since the Great Revolution, had taught the necessity of inaugurating a workers' republic, and of accomplishing this end, if necessary, by revolutionary means.

From this twofold opposition arose an acute problem for the liberal republicans. If, as could hardly be denied, the liberal Republic was revolutionary in origin, at what point did the right to revolution cease? Put in its simplest terms, if republicans had the right to overthrow dynastic regimes, did socialists have the right to overthrow the *bourgeois* Republic?

Renouvier's answer to this question was that revolutionary means were justified in order to overthrow undemocratic or dictatorial states and to install a liberal republic, but not for any other purpose. " If," he wrote, " the acts of a government are arbitrary, unjust and tyrannical, so that it ceases to be of use to society; if that government, representing an oppressive minority, reveals itself as an enemy of the state, which it is leading to ruin, then conscience pronounces a *casus belli* and passes to the side of insurrection." [23] The *raison d'être* of revolution, in other words, was to free the people from tyranny, not to inaugurate socialism.

Renouvier's statement was not directed merely against the royalist and Bonapartist regimes that had governed nineteenth century France; the ' oppressive minority ' to which he referred

23 " Les conditions de moralité des insurrections," *Critique philosophique,* 1872, I, 120 ff.

was the principal target of his attack. By this group he understood that narrow *bourgeois* oligarchy which had held the
dominant position in French society since the Great Revolution, and which has been referred to above as the dynastic
bourgeoisie. Renouvier pointed out—and it is a contention
quite central to the understanding of his whole republican position—that this oligarchy constituted only a *section* of the
middle class, albeit a very rich and influential one, and by no
means the middle class as a whole.[24] This group was virtually
a caste of wealthy families, army officers, and high clerics; its
interests in the past had in many ways been opposed to those
of the rest of society.[25]

Renouvier attacked this section of the *bourgeoisie* in the bit-
terest of terms;[26] ever since the Jacobin episode in the Great
Revolution it had identified republicanism with mass rule and
popular violence,[27] and had therefore repudiated the republican
idea and sought by other means to maintain its class rule and
to protect its special privileges. It had turned to the traditional,
hereditary monarchy to restore the stable conditions which it
sought, supporting first the Bourbon and then the Orleanist
branch of the royal family. But the old monarchy had been
powerless to help the oligarchy; the Crown had received its
death-blow from the principles of '89, and in the historical
conditions prevailing in France in the nineteenth century, had
lost any chance of taking root, of again becoming a permanent
social institution. Royalism in 1870, added Pillon, was a contingent, empirical solution to the state question and could not

24 The original phrase is *une partie de la classe moyenne.* "Les internationales et la bourgeoisie," *Critique philosophique,* 1872, II, 323.

25 "Des progrès du mépris et de ses causes," *Critique philosophique,* 1872,
I, 113 ff.

26 Renouvier's estimate of the dynastic *bourgeoisie* was made in "Des
progrès du mépris et de ses causes," an extremely perspicacious historical
essay that appeared in the *Critique philosophique* of March 14 and 28, 1872.

27 "La doctrine républicaine," *Critique philosophique,* 1872, II, 3.

be justified by political theory. Its governmental forms were not adapted to the post-revolutionary *milieu*.[28]

In 1848, continued Renouvier, the monarchy had been swept away; a Republic based upon universal suffrage had been set up. The oligarchy had been faced with the prospect of losing the monopoly of political power which it had enjoyed virtually uninterrupted since 1815. In this situation it had run full tilt into the arms of a 'saviour of society' in the person of Napoleon III. The latter personified the return of dictatorship, of Caesarism, in its most corrupt and vulgar form; but Caesarism, no more than the monarchy, could provide a solution of the state question and satisfaction for the interests of the oligarchy. Napoleon, it is true, violently suppressed the republican party and the democratic movement; but he took the road of military adventure which ended finally in national defeat and revolution.

At the time, in 1872, when Renouvier was penning his indictment of the oligarchy, the latter had just committed what was, in his eyes, the last and most enormous of its crimes. Under the leadership of Adolphe Thiers and the Versailles Assembly it had consummated the bloody repression of the Paris *Commune*. With this deed in mind Renouvier castigated the dynastic *bourgeoisie* for " a disposition to employ violence, extreme injustice in its judgments, a blind passion for reaction, and an impudent scorn for the principles of law and order." [29]

The group to which Renouvier referred used violence against the popular republican movement in 1871 precisely because the latter challenged its continued control and domination of the state. It ruled France from 1871 to 1875 through the Ver-

28 " Le dilemme: Césarisme ou République," *Critique philosophique*, 1872, I, 371 ff. Renouvier and Pillon were not concerned to explain why, after the French Revolution, traditional hereditary monarchy was impossible as a permanent form of government in France. It sufficed for them to state this as a fact.

29 " Les internationales et la bourgeoisie," *Critique philosophique, op. cit.*, 323.

sailles Assembly, continuing during this period to suppress the republican movement and to intrigue for the restoration of a royalist regime. It was precisely against these people that Renouvier considered revolutionary action to be justified. He considered that the oligarchy was attempting to usurp functions and powers that belonged to society at large and that for this purpose it had not hesitated to ally itself with the most brutal royalist and Caesarist reaction.

Renouvier's antagonism to the oligarchy was based upon one fundamental point. He thought that in the industrial era when the masses were pressing forward and becoming politically conscious it was inconceivable that a small section of the *bourgeoisie* could continue to monopolize state power. In the era of democracy there could be " only one kind of monarchy, Caesarism, and one form only of the free state, the republic." Dictatorship or republic, this was the dilemma of the modern age; society must make its choice.

Insurrections to Renouvier were thus legitimate insofar as they freed society from a dictatorial or other undemocratic regime, and insofar as they produced institutions that would legally represent the people's will, viz., a republic based upon universal suffrage. But this statement by no means involved the position that the people *themselves* should rule; " on the contrary," he wrote, " the people will not for a long time to come find themselves in this position." Renouvier, somewhat uncritically, included all popular movements under the term Jacobinism; he identified the latter with mob violence, and, in his mature years,[30] showed a most uncompromising hostility towards it. Jacobinism, which he characterized as " the violent and arbitrary action of determined minorities," he feared because it seemed to him to challenge the liberal Republic and to sanction the direct intervention of the people in public affairs.[31] Revolutionary initiative from this source he repudiated.

30 His Jacobin tendencies and writings during the Revolution of 1848 Renouvier later characterized as a *péché de jeunesse.*

31 " De l'intrusion des foules dans le gouvernement," *Critique philosophique,* 1872, II, 197 ff.

In this respect he assumed completely the position of the Girondists during the Great Revolution, and in many historical writings castigated the Jacobins for their violence and their role in rousing the people against duly constituted, sovereign assemblies.[32]

Repudiating the role of the people in government, Renouvier insisted that the *bourgeoisie* alone contained the elements from which the nation's rulers must be selected. Positive *bourgeois* virtues, he said, included "respect for rights and obligations, regard for national traditions and customs, sincere attachment to the rule of law, and the observation of moderation in all things."[33] For this reason, he added, the last word in revolutionary movements and the principal role in popular leadership must inevitably belong to "*men who possess goods, intelligence and talents.* . . ."[34]

The contradiction between these statements and Renouvier's condemnation of the corrupt and incapable *bourgeois* oligarchy that had been dominant in French society for the better part of the nineteenth century was only apparent. To his way of thinking, as we have seen, the oligarchy constituted merely a reactionary section of the *bourgeois* class. The latter, taken as a whole, contained men of reason, moderation and ability. These, the men of 'right reason,' constituted 'a natural aristocracy' in French society, "a natural and legitimate one to the extent that it results from the admitted inequality of intelligence and talent. . . ." It was such men that the people, in the liberal Republic, would designate to rule the country. Democracy and the principle of aristocracy were hence quite compatible to Renouvier; the aristocratic principle thus understood was, he considered, quite indispensable to good govern-

---

32 For example, the crisis of May 31, 1793 when the people rose under Jacobin leadership and drove the Girondists from the Assembly he characterized as "the mutilation of a sovereign legislative authority consummated at the hands of the most ardent republicans." *Ibid.*, 199.

33 "Les internationales et la bourgeoisie," *op. cit.*, 323.

34 Italics not in original.

ment.[35] Liberal republicans were the men of 'right reason,' qualified by virtue of education and ability to act for the less informed members of society with the consent, choice and approval of the latter.[36]

Hence, in the last resort, the liberal Republic signified to Renouvier the rule of the propertied class as a whole, not merely of the dynastic, or royalist, section of that class. But, once the Republic had been set up, the era of revolution was over, and social progress must henceforth be achieved by pacific means only. Further resort to force could under no conditions be justified.

IV

According to Renouvier the liberal *bourgeoisie* as a whole was to exercize state power through the institutions of a republic. He found the legal basis of the state in the consent, perpetually renewed, of the individuals composing it. In his youth, and strongly under the influence of Rousseau, he had been in favor of direct democracy, believing that sovereignty was essentially an attribute of the individual and as such indelegable.[37] Later he became convinced that such a system was impracticable for nation-states such as France;[38] representative government was the only alternative, and delegation of authority must be based upon universal suffrage. Under this democratic arrangement the sovereign individual would enter into the untramelled enjoyment of his natural rights.

35 *Science de la morale, op. cit.*, II, 211, 212.

36 This conception of political leadership was quite opposed to that of Ernest Renan, whose idea of a *cultural élite* was based, in the last resort, upon tradition and divorced from popular control. Picard, *Philosophie sociale, op. cit.*, 119 fn.

37 Renouvier developed this thesis in his *Organisation centrale et communale de la République* (Paris, 1851) : at this date he conceived of France as a federation of autonomous 'canton-communes,' each directed by its own assembly.

38 Picard, *Philosophie sociale, op. cit.*, 139.

But here a problem at once arose. The liberal Republic was to be based upon the leadership and the predominance of property-holders. Society, in addition, contained propertyless classes in the form of landless farm laborers and of an industrial proletariat. In other words privilege and poverty existed side by side, and conflict was therefore bound to occur. Renouvier was driven inescapably to the conclusion that the Republic must to some extent be a repressive state. It must organize its forces not merely to guarantee the nation against foreign attack but to safeguard the rights of property as well. A way, in other words, must be found to justify the republican state as a centralized organization armed with repressive powers and laws.

This conclusion negated Renouvier's previous contention that *bourgeois* leaders could be found, guided by the moral law and ' right reason,' to run the affairs of the state with the consent and approval of all the governed. He reached a solution to this problem by making a distinction between ' the state of peace' and ' the state of war.' Renouvier considered that, ideally, society would be based upon the full sovereignty of the individual and the free play of natural rights. In such a society all men would be fully rational and would voluntarily fulfil their obligations to one another and to the group as a whole. There would be no need for a state, conceived as a special organization distinct from society itself. Order and peace would prevail.[39]

Under actual conditions this ideal state did not and could not prevail. The actual state of society, with its class and international conflicts, Renouvier termed ' the state of war.' [40] From the existence of the latter Renouvier deduced a concept termed the right of defense; upon this, in turn, he based the twin institutions of private property and the state.

39 In all this Renouvier's indebtedness to Proudhon is evident.

40 Renouvier's ideas on the state of war and its implications for political theory are clearly expounded by Hamelin, *Le Système de Renouvier*, *op. cit.*, 387-401.

The right of defense took both individual and collective forms. At its simplest it was equivalent to defense against physical attack, but this was not, in Renouvier's eyes, its most important element. He considered, on the contrary, that property was the most valuable instrument that a man could dispose of in order to protect himself against the exploitation of others; and he defined it as "an instrument of defense against social injustice." [41] Property, he believed, in conformity with the *philosophes,* was a natural right, acceptable to reason as a guarantee of individual freedom against economic domination or enslavement by others. A veritable extension of the human personality, it expressed the right of all members of society to have independent means for the attainment of personal aims without having to depend on anyone else and without being at their mercy.[42]

Property, then, was the most important *individual* form taken by the right of defense. Its fundamental *collective* form was the state: the latter arose because men in the state of war were driven to unite one with another for mutual protection. Society's right over its members was, Renouvier said, nothing more than the collective exercize of the individual's right to self-defense. Clearly, what each had a right to do on his own all had a right to do together. The state of war and the consequent right of a group to take measures for its own defense resulted in the introduction of constraint into the concept and practice of law. Violence was permissible, under the given historical conditions, to ensure the sanctity of property and the preservation of society. The main purpose of the state, therefore, was to organize measures to guarantee the protection of society on the one hand and the maintenance of individual rights—and especially property rights—on the other.

The republic as a state favoring the dominance of the *bourgeoisie* and protecting the interests of the property-holders in-

41 "Du droit personnel de défense," *Critique philosophique,* 1872, II, 293.

42 For his ideas concerning property Renouvier was indebted as much to Proudhon as to the eighteenth century.

dividually and collectively, such is the concept that emerges with great precision from Renouvier's thought. But Renouvier also understood that the mere repression of those who challenged the rights of private property was inadequate to secure the future of the *bourgeois* Republic. The existence of a propertyless class, deprived of independent means of subsistence, was clearly incompatible with the continuation of such a regime, regardless of the degree of repression which the latter exercized.

He therefore cast about for some means to redress the balance so heavily weighted in favor of the property-owner. He found it, he thought, in the idea of association. Association of the propertyless, borrowed, as we have seen, from Charles Fourier and Louis Blanc, was complementary in his system to property as a guarantee of individual freedom; it would, he considered, take the form of producers cooperatives, mutual aid societies and trade unions. Such associations, he thought, could alone compensate the people for the deprivations which they suffered under the existing system. Association was the democratic liberty *par excellence* and imposed strict limits to the power which the state or other groups could exercize over the members of society.[43]

For the major part of the nineteenth century in France, until the trade-union Act of 1884, working-class organization was specifically forbidden by law. Benefit societies, it is true, were tolerated during this period, on the grounds that they diminished proletarian distress and hence revolutionary trends. But attempts at unionization were for the most part ruthlessly punished. Renouvier's insistence on the working-class' right of association reflected the conviction of liberal republicans that a repressive policy in this respect was, no more than the maintenance of a restrictive franchise, compatible with the conditions of the new industrial age: it constituted a significant revision of traditional Girondist ideas.

43 One of the best articles developing the neo-Girondist position on working-class organization was written by François Pillon under the title " La liberté d'association," *Critique philosophique*, 1872, I, 39 ff.

V

Renouvier, in common with almost all republicans since Condorcet's time, had faith in the power of reason to change and to improve men's minds. Education, he thought, was a necessary instrument with which to lay the foundations of a republican state; lacking instruction, neither peasants nor workers could develop those associations upon which, according to the neo-Girondists, their economic strength would depend; nor would they be equipped to take their places as citizens in a regime supposedly based upon popular sovereignty and operated by and for the people.

Between the republicans and the realization of this ideal stood the Church. The idea of popular, compulsory, mass education in France came originally from the Calvinist movement in the sixteenth century.[44] It had been one of the aims of the Huguenots to destroy the influence of Catholic dogma in the schools and to impart to the nation a degree of literacy upon which the study of the Bible might be based. The collapse of the early Protestant movement had left the Church in undisputed control [45] of the educational system, a situation which continued substantially unchanged well into the nineteenth century. The Great Revolution, it is true, carried out great ecclesiastical changes, but it hardly shook the age-old clerical monopoly of popular instruction. Beginning with the *Concordat* of 1801 the Church had actually begun to strengthen a position undermined by twelve years of revolution and civil war: officially or unofficially the religious orders returned to the country, from which they had previously been expelled, and new missions were founded. By the end of the Restoration Catholicism had won back, by devious means, no small part of the ghostly influence which it had enjoyed in pre-revolutionary

44 See Guillaume Farel, *De l'instruction des enfants* (Geneva, 1552).

45 This statement must be qualified by reference to the Jansenist movement, which during the eighteenth century effectively challenged the Church's propagation of accepted dogmas.

days, and this state of affairs was not seriously challenged during the subsequent dynastic period. Possessing a virtual monopoly of private education, clerical influence was also entrenched in the rudimentary public system established by the first Napoleon.[46]

And yet, it would be a mistake to conclude that at the time of the Revolution the Church's position in respect to education had not undergone a significant change. When the men of '89 destroyed monarchical absolutism the Church became the most powerful surviving representative of the royalist regime and its traditions. No longer a mere ally of the French autocracy, it stood forth now as the last stronghold of the authoritarian principle. In the nineteenth century dynasties came and went, weak and ephemeral things that possessed little beyond the shadow of power and were sloughed off rapidly. Feeling their own weakness and instability, these successive regimes all leaned heavily upon the Church.

Ecclesiastical influence over society was, for the most part, exercized through the Catholic monopoly of schools and teachers. It was for this reason that republican criticism focussed upon clerical control of education. Whereas before the Revolution Catholic instruction had been one among many buttresses of Bourbon absolutism, after the Revolution it became the principle obstacle to the development of liberal republican institutions and ideas and, therefore, the principal target of republican attack.

Renouvier produced one of the clearest statements of the neo-Girondist position with respect to Catholicism and educational reform.[47] He contended that the Republic must step in

46 Clerical influence in education reached its height after the passage of the Falloux Law in 1850.

47 Renouvier's position is summarized in Weill, *Histoire de l'idée laique*, *op. cit.*, 228-233. His criticism of Catholic education and ideas on educational reform are expressed in " L'éducation et la morale," *Critique philosophique*, 1872, I, 273-280; " Les réformes de l'instruction publique," *ibid.*, 1872, II, 161-167; and " La réforme des études classiques," *ibid.*, 1872, II, 177-184.

to fill the gap created by the absence of a public education system, and must provide those services that "the Church cannot and will not furnish, and which it does not want anybody else to furnish in its stead."

In principle, as a step toward this end, Renouvier advocated separation of Church and state; Catholics, he thought, should be free to continue teaching their own morality and practicing their own cult, but they should no longer be supported for these purposes from the public treasury. Disestablishment was to him " just, necessary, and simply a question of time." [48] However, Renouvier opposed immediate separation of Church and state on the grounds that the former, subject to endowment and regulation, would provide less embarrassment for the Republic than if left entirely free and uncontrolled.[49] He considered that the real defense against clericalism lay, not in attacking the Church under the concordatory regime, but in developing education as a weapon of republican enlightenment. The state had, in his opinion, not only a right but a duty to conduct its own propaganda and to inculcate its own ideas. " Civic education," he wrote, ". . . effectively propagated, will deliver men's souls from the yoke of theocracy. . . ." [50]

For these reasons Renouvier considered that the Third Republic must carry forward in the educational field the work of emancipation from the Church which had been begun by the First Republic. The establishment of a state school system, the banishment of religious teaching from all but specifically sectarian schools, and, finally, the disestablishment of Church and state, were to him necessary measures with which to complete the original revolutionary effort. These measures sprang from the very nature of the republican position, which demanded the final subordination of Catholicism if the institutions of the liberal Republic were to survive in France.

48 " Le catholicisme et l'état," *Critique philosophique*, 1872, II, 391.

49 *Ibid.*, 390, 391.

50 *Ibid.*, 393.

Renouvier thought that state schools might serve as vehicles of republican propaganda, but he certainly did not believe that they could of themselves emancipate France from the grip of the Catholic faith. His hostility to the latter sprang from a rejection of the authoritarian principles of the Church and the dogmatic bases of its morality. France, he wrote, must either overcome this 'slave-religion' or society itself would perish.[51]

Renouvier, in holding this position, was not adopting an anti-religious attitude. He desired merely to combat Catholicism by another faith that was more in accordance with the needs of the times; and such a faith he considered was available in Protestantism.[52] The latter had, he considered, many advantages: "it need not," he wrote, "violate its principles in order to live in peace with science on the one side and with democracy on the other." Protestant countries had, moreover, "been disposed to see nature and history in their true light; and have submitted them to criticism and have studied the normal development of historical fact instead of accepting ready-made, arbitrary or traditional opinion." [53]

But Renouvier pointed out that Protestant teaching was insufficiently known in France. The long centuries of Protestant persecution were regarded as a matter of indifference, as so much of the dead and forgotten past; the struggles of the great reformers, the 'infamy and horror' of their martyrdom, did not move liberals as they should. The French reformed Churches were weak and poor by comparison with the Catholic organization.[54]

---

51 *Correspondance de Renouvier et Secrétan* (Paris, 1910), 58.

52 Renouvier considered that any idea of reforming Catholicism must be set aside. The clerical organization and the theocracy which it served was staffed by an army of priests no more prepared to submit to reform than three centuries previously. "Notre programme," *La Critique religieuse, première année* (1878), 1.

53 *Ibid.*, 2.

54 Renouvier described the French Church as "a sort of central fortress for the defense of the privileges which the rich *bourgeoisie* enjoys." *Ibid.*, 3.

It was as a move in what he considered an inevitable struggle with Catholicism that Renouvier in 1878 founded a quarterly review entitled *The Critique of Religion*.[55] The purpose of this journal, he stated, was to promote a truer understanding of Protestantism. The growth of the latter would, he claimed, " help the social development of peoples with Latin, Catholic and Caesarist traditions." *The Critique of Religion* continued publication for twelve years; but its influence upon liberal republicans was negligible.[56] The idea of making Protestantism triumphant in France in the era of the Third Republic was a ridiculously utopian one, and it is strange that Renouvier should not have realized this. But this journalistic experiment is of real significance in evaluating Renouvier's liberal thought itself, and in establishing the historical tradition to which it was related. Renouvier was fully aware of the similarity that existed between the ideals of the sixteenth century reformers and their nineteenth century republican successors. Both combated the social supremacy of the Catholic Church and attacked its doctrines in the name of conscience, judgment and human reason. Renouvier's effort, furthermore, to associate the Republic with Protestantism as a means of weakening the Church reflected a definite trend among the opportunists in the late 1870's and early 1880's. Protestants at this time occupied a position of influence in the liberal party out of all proportion to their numerical strength in the country at large; and it was they who were largely responsible for the education laws of the years 1879 to 1882 which constituted the principle neo-Girondist contribution toward the strengthening of the republican regime.[57]

55 *La Critique religieuse, supplément trimestriel de la Critique philosophique.* This review attracted a number of well-known Protestant contributors. It is a mine of information on sixteenth as well as nineteenth century history.

56 Weill, *Histoire de l'idée laique, op. cit.,* 233.

57 This point is well made by Evelyn M. Acomb, *The French Laic Laws 1879-1889* (New York, 1941), 55, 56.

VI

The extent of Renouvier's achievement is measured by the fact that almost alone he founded the school of neo-criticism in France in the face of strongly flowing currents of positivism, eclecticism and social Darwinism;[58] and established, upon this base, a mature and systematic doctrine of liberal republicanism. Renouvier's influence upon his contemporaries was correspondingly great. From 1870 until the first World War a whole generation of French liberal republicans came, directly or indirectly, under his sway.[59] At the Sorbonne Renouvier's principles were expounded by Marion, Séailles, Michel, at the École Normale Supérieure by Brochard, at the Academy of Paris by Liard.[60] A host of philosophers expounded neo-criticism in the provinces, among whom Hamelin at Bordeaux and Dauriac at Montpellier were the best known.[61] Repre-

58 It has not been possible, within the limits of the present essay, to indicate the extent of the polemic which Renouvier conducted against these types of philosophy, in which determinism played a dominant part. "His whole work," wrote Wilfred Monod, "was dominated by the desire to protect human personality against the determinist flood." Quelques philosophes de France (Libourne, 1941), 41.

59 "One may say," wrote Prat, "that the most distinguished thinkers of the end of the nineteenth century were influenced by his thought." Charles Renouvier, op. cit., 263.

60 The work of Marion and Michel is dealt with below, 78-82. Gabriel Séailles (1852-1922) taught philosophy at the Sorbonne from 1896 until his death. He was the author, among other works, of a commentary, La Philosophie de Charles Renouvier (Paris, 1905). Victor Brochard (1848-1907) was the author of works on philosophy and logic, and a close follower of Renouvier. Louis Liard (1846-1917) made a name for himself at Bordeaux in the first years of the Republic as professor of philosophy and a municipal leader. In 1884 he was appointed Director of Higher Education at the Ministry of Public Education. Well-known as an educationist and administrator, he was also the author of numerous works on philosophy and logic, and a disciple of Renouvier and Kant.

61 Octave Hamelin (1856-1907) taught philosophy at the University of Bordeaux, and later at the Sorbonne. He was the author of a text on Renouvier's philosophical system. Lionel Dauriac (1847-1878) was appointed professor of philosophy at the University of Montpellier in 1882. He was a close collaborator of Renouvier's, contributing many articles to the

sentative of other teachers influenced by Renouvier were the famous legist Beudant [62] and the professor of medicine Dupuy.[63] Among the younger men who began to exercize an influence during this period, and whose activities were to continue throughout the era of the Third Republic, and even into the Fourth, mention may be made of Picard.[64]

Toward the end of the nineteenth century the program and philosophy of liberal republicanism began to lose its vitality in France. It was subjected to a three-fold assault simultaneously at the hands of the royalists, the radical republicans and the socialists. Neo-Girondism was able to hold its own neither as a political nor as a philosophic force. After the turn of the century it was supplanted by more advanced neo-Jacobin and *Sansculotte* parties and programs.

Yet the liberal tradition, if forced to give ground to its more radical republican opponents, remained a powerful force until

---

Critique philosophique. He also taught at the Sorbonne. One of Renouvier's principal followers, he was the author of many philosophical works and wrote a standard short exposition of Renouvier's philosophy for the *Grande Encyclopédie* under the title of *Criticisme.*

62 Charles Beudant (1829-1905) was a professor of law who became Dean of the Faculty of Law in Paris in 1879. A moderate republican in politics, he was a fanatical opponent of state intervention in social life, which he regarded as a restriction upon the rights of the individual. He exercized a great influence in the teaching of law, his best known work being *Le Droit individuel et l'État* (Paris, 1891).

63 Paul Dupuy (1827-?), member of an old-established Protestant family in the Dordogne, became in 1864 a professor of medicine at the University of Bordeaux. A philosopher as well as a doctor, he wrote many works expounding and popularizing the principles of liberal republicanism and of republican morality.

64 Roger Picard (1884-) made his *début* at the age of twenty-four with the brilliant commentary *La Philosophie sociale de Renouvier*, the preparation of which, as he recounted later, "strengthened my democratic convictions." From 1910 until the outbreak of the World War Picard taught at the *École Supérieure de Commerce* in Paris, and subsequently at the University of Lille and the Sorbonne. He was the author during this period of various works on economics and law. Picard produced in 1944 a somewhat truncated statement of liberal republican principles, *La Démocratie française.*

the outbreak of the first World War. Renouvier's republican system received further development and a more concise formulation preeminently in the works of Marion, Michel and the Swiss philosopher Secrétan. All three men made important contributions to which some attention must now be given. The work that they did was more than merely the sterile elaboration of a philosophy which had passed the height of its influence and was now on the decline. These writers, in addition to Renouvier, deeply influenced the radical-socialist philosophy of *solidarité* which was, after the turn of the century, to supplant neo-Girondism as a quasi-official republican creed. *Solidarité*, in a very real sense, developed out of the theories elaborated by Renouvier and his leading followers.

Henri Marion (1846-1896) had a career as teacher and writer that was almost exactly coincidental with the first quarter of a century of the Third Republic and with the dominance in political and intellectual life of the liberal republican trend. Marion started his career in 1868 as a teacher of philosophy in the provinces, first at Pau and then at Bordeaux. Taking up an appointment at Paris in 1875, he played an active part, after 1880, in organizing secondary education as a member of the *Conseil supérieur de l'instruction publique*. From 1883 until the end of his life he taught the theory of education at the Sorbonne. Marion was a man of colossal industry who exercized a manifold influence upon contemporary intellectuals. He was a close disciple of Renouvier's and considered that the spreading of the liberal republican philosophy was a central part of his life's work.[65] He was also director of the Philosophy and Education section of the *Grande Encyclopédie*, an enterprise to which he contributed numerous articles. After 1880, indeed, Marion was considered preeminent among the liberal republicans of his time as philosopher, publicist and educator.

---

65 " It is," he wrote, " the reading of Renouvier that has inspired my work...." *De la solidarité morale* (Paris, 1880), 2 fn.

Marion's first work, published in 1878, was a study of John Locke;[66] thereafter until his death he produced various studies on education and morals. But his most enduring work, and one that was to have a major influence upon subsequent republican philosophers, was the *Treatise on Moral Solidarity* published in 1880.[67] Here Marion developed and popularized Renouvier's theme that the basis of social cohesion lay in the individual's sense of unity with and dependance upon the other members of society. He applied this concept to the elucidation of various types of human relationship and to the study of history. But Marion, in elaborating Renouvier's position, in no way went beyond it. Progress, in his opinion, came as the result of individual decisions to do good, not from any social struggle or collective action; and thus to his way of thinking social evils, and industrial exploitation in particular, could be remedied neither by the neo-Jacobin idea of social legislation, nor by the *Sansculotte* advocacy of collectivism. His philosophy reaffirmed the *laissez-faire* position that improvement in the conditions of life could be attained only by the exercize of Christian charity, and by the recognition of a purely personal, charitable relationship between rich and poor. Marion's neo-Jacobin successors, as we shall see, were to reject such concepts in favor of a social solidarity based upon the division of labor as opposed to a moral solidarity based upon mere feelings. But Marion's work played no small part in initiating the development of a concept that was to become after the turn of the century a household word in France.

The greatest of Renouvier's disciples was Henry Michel.[68] Michel (1857-1904) died at the height of his powers while still quite a young man. He resembled Marion in enjoying a

66 *John Locke, sa vie et son œuvre* (Paris, 1878).

67 *De la solidarité morale, op. cit.*

68 Much interesting biographical material and commentary will be found in the series of articles and obituary notices collected under the title *Henry Michel* (Paris, n. d.). See also Roger Soltau, "Henry Michel," in the *Encyclopedia of the Social Sciences* (New York, 1933), X, 403, 404.

teaching and writing career that was coincidental with the apogée of liberal republicanism between the years 1875 and 1900. Michel became in 1882 an editor of the journal *Le Temps*, to which he contributed articles for many years.[69] This activity, together with his work in founding the *Société de l'histoire de la Révolution de 1848*, brought him into close contact with many leading republicans, notably Jules Ferry, Léon Bourgeois, Edouard Millerand, Alfred Dreyfus, Jean Jaurès, and others. But his reputation as an original thinker and republican *idéologue* was made only a few years before his death with the publication in 1895 of his treatise on *The Concept of the State*, a monumental work surveying the entire development of French political thought in the nineteenth century.[70] In 1896 a special chair was created for Michel at the Sorbonne in the history of political theory; and it was there, until his death in 1904, that he gave a series of courses on the evolution of French democratic thought. These courses were based upon a vast amount of original research. In giving them Michel demonstrated great scholarly capacities and the ability to master and organise an impressive array of original material.[71]

Michel found in Renouvier before all others the inspiration for his life and teaching. Lucien Lévy-Bruhl, the famous historian of French philosophy and Michel's lifelong friend and

69 These articles were collected in *Le Quarantième Fauteuil* (Paris, 1898), and *Propos de morale* (Paris, 1904-1905).

70 *L'Idée de l'État, essai critique sur l'histoire des théories sociales et politiques en France depuis la Révolution* (Paris, 1895).

71 Of this period of Michel's life, Alfred Rebelliau wrote: " Not once, in eight years, did he consider taking up again a subject that he had already dealt with. And yet the preparation of a new topic ... was an enormous task. Usually he had to go right back to the texts—to the works of political writers, to the parliamentary debates and journals; he had to pass incessantly from the analysis of his research to exposition and synthesis ...." *Henry Michel, op. cit.*, 24, 25. It is a pity that the notes upon which Michel based his lectures were never published. They unquestionably contain material of great significance for the historian of French republican and democratic thought in the first three-quarters of the nineteenth century.

colleague, wrote that the power of Renouvier's ideas convinced Michel while he was still a young man, and he remained faithful to them throughout.[72] Indeed, Renouvier on his deathbed designated Michel as the man most worthy and most fit to carry on his neo-criticist philosophical traditions.[73]

In a little work published in 1901 and entitled *La Doctrine politique de la démocratie* Michel attempted to express in a concise and systematic form the essential elements of Renouvier's liberal republican theory.[74] The purpose of this work, Michel pointed out, was to provide a statement that might be used in the struggle with rival political philosophies. The book itself was probably the most succinct statement of the neo-Girondist ideal that any French writer achieved. In it the antecedents of this creed were clearly indicated. The eighteenth century, said Michel, handed down the germs of the doctrine, and substantial contributions to its development were made by such pioneers of democratic thought as Michelet, Quinet, Proudhon, and de Tocqueville. But the fully elaborated philosophy, together with its characteristic techniques of analysis, were first propounded by Renouvier. Michel described the *Science de la morale* as " one of the finest works on moral and political philosophy ever written." The *Critique philosophique,* in similar vein, he characterized as " a political catechism for the use of democracies." [75]

72 *Henry Michel, op. cit.,* 7-10, and J. E. Roberty, *ibid.,* 3.

73 *Les Derniers Entretiens,* recorded by Louis Prat (Paris, 1904), 106.

74 Apart from this work, and that on the theory of the state previously mentioned, Michel's most important contribution consisted of a study *La Loi Falloux,* published posthumously in 1906. Michel's works are listed in full in the bibliography.

75 *La Doctrine politique de la démocratie* (Paris, 1901), 22. He added: " I do not know any document of greater value than the *Critique philosophique* for whoever will one day attempt to write the history of political and moral ideas in the last third of the nineteenth century." *Loc. cit.*—an estimate with which the present writer in part agrees.

Michel's brochure, brilliant as it was in style and statement, was in essence no more than a condensation of Renouvier's leading ideas; it added nothing new to the now traditional concept of French liberal democracy. Michel, in accordance with this, the classical *bourgeois* tradition, presented democracy as preeminently a political, not an economic, concept. Political liberty,—that is, freedom of conscience, thought, speech, press and assembly—respect for law, for pacific as opposed to revolutionary change, for popular sovereignty expressed through universal manhood suffrage, such was the quintessence of Michel's ideal. It was on the one side a glowing defense of political equality, but on the other a calm acceptance of economic inequality:

> "Real equality," [he wrote] "equality of fact, in virtue of which all citizens should have the same lot, the same advantages, this is not in the program of any true democrat. Never has democracy promised to level heads or even fortunes. All that it tries to do is to develop social institutions in such a way that there is less inequality at the point of departure of individual destinies." [76]

La Doctrine politique de la démocratie was, in effect, no more than a bold restatement of a waning cause. Its publication is significant because it marked the end of one era of republican thought and indicated the point of departure from which the new republican generation would move forward to the elaboration of more advanced social and political ideas.

No account of French liberal republicanism would be complete without mention of the work of the Swiss philosopher Charles Secrétan. Secrétan, who was a lifelong friend of Renouvier, greatly elaborated the associationist side of his French colleague's work. Subsequent republican generations were to draw heavily upon Secrétan's analysis to justify their arguments in favor of state legislative intervention in the interests of the dispossessed.

76 *Ibid.*, 48, 49.

Charles Secrétan (1815-1895)[77] came from a well-to-do and long-established Protestant family of Lausanne. Part of his youth he spent in a wandering student life, attending the universities of Stuttgart and Munich—at the latter he sat at the feet of the venerable Friedrich Schelling—and torn between the rival attractions of philosophy, journalism and law. Finally in 1841 Secrétan settled down in Lausanne as professor of philosophy at the Academy there and began to contribute articles to the paper *Le Semeur,* at that time one of the leading organs of French Protestantism. In one of these articles he reviewed Renouvier's *Manuel de philosophie moderne,* which appeared in 1842, and thus introduced it to both Swiss and French readers.

In 1849 Secrétan published his first major work, *Le Philosophie de la liberté,* which summarized his philosophic and religious teachings of the previous years. This work, which made his reputation in Switzerland, was a philosophy of religion and of history. Rationalist in method, idealist in approach, it was largely influenced by Descartes and Kant and in fundamentals resembled the neo-Kantian philosophy that was, more or less contemporaneously, being elaborated by Renouvier. Secrétan, in the best traditions of liberal and Protestant theory, exalted the rights of the individual, the sacredness of conscience, the reality of human freedom and moral choice.[78]

In 1850 Secrétan transferred to Neuchâtel, where he spent the next sixteen years. During this period his religious interests, with their primitive, evangelical quality, remained up-

77 The most useful general source for Secrétan's life and work is Louise Secrétan, *Charles Secrétan, sa vie et son œuvre* (Paris, 4th edition, 1912). This book prints in full or quotes copiously from much of Secrétan's private correspondence, articles, etc. The reader is referred to it for full information concerning Secrétan's various publications.

78 Secrétan's philosophy had a firm theological basis. Man's fall to him was real, and human progress, incontestable. History was a work of " restoration," of moral recovery.

permost;[79] but with the approach of the Third Republic in France and the breaking of the international crisis of 1870-1871 his interest in speculative philosophy began to wane. After 1870 he abandoned the pursuit of metaphysics and devoted the rest of his life to the study of the social question. This shifting of interest coincided with the development of a close friendship and collaboration with Renouvier. The two philosophers had entered into correspondence in 1868 and the exchange continued for a quarter of a century.[80] If Secrétan began to elaborate reformist ideas that were near to the heart of Renouvier, his own direct influence upon the French philosopher was marked; the latter, from this time on, began to incline noticeably towards Protestantism. Secrétan's influence upon French liberal republicanism in general became most marked toward the end of the century. The pages of the *Critique philosophique* were open to him for the development of his views;[81] he began to find followers and imitators in many French universities as a result of personal contacts, of the books which he wrote, and of the many articles which he published in both Swiss and French religious and philosophic magazines.[82] Secrétan thus became an acknowledged spokesman in France for the type of Christian socialism which had been adumbrated but not completely developed in Renouvier's writings.

79 Of Secrétan and his friend Bovet at this time Louise Secrétan wrote: "They experienced the same religious needs, the same yearnings after saintliness, the same anguish at not having attained it, the same feeling of sin, the same thirst for pardon." Louise Secrétan, *op. cit.*, 282.

80 See the *Correspondance de Renouvier et Secrétan, op. cit.* Concerning this exchange Secrétan's daughter wrote: "By means of the pen a profound and complete intimacy was established." Louise Secrétan, *op. cit.*, 400.

81 "You cannot exaggerate," wrote Raoul Allier, one of Renouvier's disciples, "the role of Renouvier in making known Secrétan." Quoted by Louise Secrétan, *op. cit.*, 449.

82 Notably *La Révue chrétienne, Évangile et liberté,* and *La Révue philosophique.*

Secrétan's social thought was expressed with greatest force-fulness in *Études sociales*, a collection of articles for various learned journals that was published at Lausanne in 1889.[83] Here he depicted the miseries of proletarian life and showed how the existence of an oppressed class led to conflicts that threatened to disrupt capitalist society. He traced at length the origins of contemporary social evils and found an explanation of them in the fact that land, originally the property of the entire community, had been divided up and converted out-right into private property "by a series of usurpations and encroachments." The perpetuation of this theft produced a class deprived of independent means of support and compelled to work for the benefit of others.

Secrétan defined the social question as the investigation of the means whereby this situation might be remedied. He would have liked to have solved it in the traditional utopian fashion, by trying somehow to extend private property to all, and hence *abolishing* the proletariat.[84] His social program was, therefore, little more than a repetition of the ideas of Fourier, Blanc and St. Simon with regard to the ways in which the workers might acquire capital and transform themselves into "self-employing capitalists." The principle steps toward this end were, in his opinion, the development of profit-sharing [85] and of producers' cooperatives.[86] Secrétan was not at all sure what role the state should play in accelerating this process, in which he envisaged that associations of "worker-owners" would gradually replace traditional capitalist enterprise; but, never

---

83 See also *Mon utopie: nouvelles études morales et sociales* (Paris and Lausanne, 1892) ; and *La Civilization et la croyance* (Paris, 1892).

84 "We are seeking," he wrote, "a means of abolishing (*remplacer*) the proletariat ... and we are championing for all men some sort of property without which freedom is not possible." *Études sociales, op. cit.,* 119.

85 For Secrétan's ideas on profit-sharing, see *Études sociales,* 125-159; and, for a critique of this concept, Paul Lafargue, "La participation," *Égalité,* April 16, 23 and 30, 1882.

86 *Études sociales, op. cit.,* 116, 117.

abandoning the neo-Girondist principles of the sacredness of property rights and of *laissez-faire,* he emphatically repudiated the idea that the state should in any way intervene in economic life either to carry out collectivist ideals [87] or in the interest of regulating conditions of work. He rejected out of hand the proposal, which began to be urged with increasing vigor after 1880 by both neo-Jacobins and *Sansculottes,* that the state should step in to establish minimum wage-rates and to provide for unemployment and accident insurance.[88]

Secrétan's type of social philosophy was by the end of the century quite out of fashion in France. The Marxists had polemized effectively against it, and had managed to demonstrate to the working class that it could not place any hopes of salvation in the old, utopian ideals. By 1900, in addition, the neo-Jacobins were developing a program of state-supported legislation along the lines which Secrétan had so emphatically rejected. His work was nonetheless useful to the spokesmen of neo-Jacobinism. It afforded a starting point for their thought and enabled them to present their social proposals as an alternative solution to the social evils which Secrétan had graphically depicted. In this respect he achieved a notable elaboration of Renouvier's analysis and pointed the way to the radical republican philosophy in which social rather than political pre-occupations were uppermost.

Not all conservative republicans could boast the systematic and well-rounded outlook which Renouvier and his school expounded among the intellectuals and in the universities. To the more empirical system of Littré and his followers some attention must now be given.

87 "Equality," he wrote, "achieved at the expense of freedom, is abhorrent to us." He added that, since production depended on the profit-stimulus, inequality was necessary for the general well-being. *Ibid.,* 96 ff.

88 *Ibid.,* 172.

CHAPTER II

ÉMILE LITTRÉ AND REPUBLICAN SOCIOLOGY

CHARLES RENOUVIER was the philosopher of liberal republicanism; Émile Littré [1] was its parliamentary guide and practical adviser. Littré was born in 1801 of Jacobin parents who passed on to him, if not their convictions, at any rate a strong belief in the necessity for republican and democratic institutions.[2] He combined a personal timidity which Dr. Johnson would have scorned with a capacity for work which the latter might well have envied. While still a very young man, Littré had achieved an extraordinary erudition, having mastered six languages, including Sanscrit, before deciding to take up medicine in 1882. However, when his father died in 1827 he abandoned the idea of becoming a doctor and turned again to linguistic pursuits as a means of earning a living. After the Revolution of 1830—when he fought on the republican side in the uniform of a National Guard—Littré joined the staff

1 The best short sketch of Littré's life, character and manifold activities is the obituary published in *Polybiblion, 2ᵉ série*, XIII (Jan.-Jul. 1881),537. The most useful of the many biographical treatments are: C. A. Sainte-Beuve, *Notice sur M. Littré, sa vie et ses travaux* (Paris, 1863); Eugène Spuller, *Figures disparues*, vol. I (Paris, 1886); and *Biographies du 19ᵉ siècle, 7ᵉ série* (Paris, 1891). Mention may also be made of Maurice Bloch, *Les Mères des grands hommes* (Paris, 1885), which stresses Littré's relations with his mother. Littré's medical contribution is dealt with in Georges Daremberg's charming study *Les Grands Médecins du 19ᵉ siècle* (Paris, 1907). An excellent critique of Littré as a positivist and in relation to the positivist movement will be found in Elme Caro, *M. Littré et le positivisme* (Paris, 1883) and the same author's "Emile Littré," *Revue des deux mondes*, L (1882), 516.

2 His mother, Sophie, was a devout Protestant from the *Lyonnais*. The royalists had shot down her father in the street during the Thermidorean reaction. Littré's father, Michel-François, was a Norman who spent his youth at sea and then settled down as a customs-official. Michel-François had a great admiration for Robespierre and named his son Maximilien after the Incorruptible.

of the newspaper *Le National,* and subsequently became one of its editors. The journalistic career upon which he thus embarked assumed the character of a literary crusade when Littré embraced Auguste Comte's philosophy in the early forties. He became at once Comte's leading French disciple, and devoted himself after 1845 to the exposition and popularization of positivism, putting out a veritable stream of articles, pamphlets and commentaries on philosophy, history and science which did not abate until after the end of the Napoleonic era. In addition to these labors Littré embarked in 1857 on his Dictionary of the French Language, a monumental work that was not completed until 1872.[3]

Littré's work as a political theorist and spokesman of the liberal republicans did not begin until his activity as a teacher of positivism was almost at an end. In 1867 he had founded a review, *La Philosophie positive,* to be the principle organ for the expression of his ideas. This journal, appearing twice monthly, played an important part in the philosophic movement of the last years of the Empire, but its character was changed considerably by the events of 1870 and 1871. From that time, until it ceased publication in 1883, its attention was given to practical politics rather than to speculative affairs. Littré himself was elected to the National Assembly in 1871 and became a member of the French Academy in the same year. Thenceforth until his death in 1882 he was recognized as one of the leading intellectual and literary figures of the Third Republic, exercizing a deep influence over the republicans both from his place in the Assembly and through his writings. " No other thinker except Renouvier," we are told, " contributed so emphatically to the shaping of the official philosophy of the Third Republic." [4] The nature of this con-

3 " Our literature," says Caro, " was endowed with a monument which will remain for all writers an indispensable aid, and which will not be surpassed for a century at least." Caro, *M. Littré et le positivisme, op. cit.,* 41 ff.

4 Réné Hubert, " Littré," *Encyclopedia of the Social Sciences,* IX, 544.

tribution, and its influence in the shaping of subsequent republican thought, are the subject of this chapter.

I

The philosophy of Auguste Comte, which underlay Littré's thought and shaped most of his ideas about society, was very popular with liberal republicans in the middle of the nineteenth century. This philosophy explained man's history in evolutionary terms and vindicated liberal ideas of scientific progress and industrial change. At the same time it made clear the meaning of the age-long struggle against both Church and Crown. Positivism taught the inevitability of advance from medieval and absolutist society to the lay, industrialized state. It thus provided a predestinarian, one might almost say Calvinistic sanction, for liberal republican aims and principles. It is, therefore, easy to understand that so clearly formulated a theory of social evoluation should have been hailed by republicans and that Littré should have first become popular by expounding it.

Reduced to its simplest terms, Comte's work consisted of a theory of science and a theory of society. The first of these was based largely upon the sensationalist psychology of Condillac and asserted that human knowledge is limited to the cognition of sense-data and to the formulation of the relationships, or laws, existing between those data. With this postulate Comte was able to dismiss metaphysics and theology as subjects of investigation, and to insist that the classification and coordination of the various scientific disciplines was alone the proper sphere of philosophical activity.

Comte's theory of society was one very significant expression of this, the so-called positivist approach to phenomena. He taught that the study of society was a scientific pursuit and that human institutions had evolved in accordance with definite and ascertainable laws.[5] Inconsistently enough, Comte adopted

5 Comte taught that society, like physics, must be analyzed in terms both of statics and dynamics; must be analyzed, that is, in terms both of its constituent parts at any one time and in terms of the process by which it had

a wholly subjective, or psychological, explanation of the factors underlying social change; the latter was, in his opinion, determined by the evolution of human ideas. Starting from this premise he asserted that the study of man's history, and that of his institutions, must be subordinated to the investigation of the changing modes of human thought. Here followed his celebrated theory of the 'three stages:' men, said Comte, explained the action of nature at first by reference to a superior creative Will. This was the theological stage of mental development. Gradually they began to understand that natural phenomena were not accidental or arbitrary occurrences, but took place in a definite and often predictable way. Accordingly they began to explain behavior by references to the ' essences ' of objects, in virtue of which these things behaved as they did. This, the ' metaphysical ' stage was finally superseded by the positivist, or scientific, when at last it began to dawn upon men that the explanation of nature must be sought in the actual sequence of phenomena themselves without reference to a suprasensory ' essence ' or ' will.' Comte drew strictly determinist conclusions from this theory. Society was evolving toward a scientific, industrial [6] age as a necessary result of the nature of things and independently of human will or effort. Like Cordorcet and St. Simon before him, he foresaw for mankind an automatic progress into an indefinite future.

After the *coup d'état* of Louis Napoleon the paths of Comte and his disciple began to diverge. The master himself rallied to the Bonapartist regime, an event which marked the beginnings of an estrangement between him and Littré. After Comte's death in 1857 this essentially political disagreement found expression in philosophical form. Littré modified his previous uncritical attitude to positivist doctrine and departed

---

evolved over a given period. Littré's strictly political writings owe their effectiveness in no small degree to the extent to which he applied both techniques to the clarification of the problems with which he was concerned.

6 Industrialism was the organization of society which in Comte's opinion corresponded to the scientific state of mind.

to some extent from his previous passionate attachment to it.[7] It was not merely that Comte had, in his old age, reverted to a "theological state of mind" where his outraged disciple could not follow him;[8] Littré had for some time been entertaining serious doubts about the law of the three stages which, it was clear, could not for long bear examination as a serious account of human intellectual development.[9] He realized also that Comte, in ignoring psychology, morals and political economy, or neglecting to relate these to his system, had failed to explain some of the more important causative factors in human history. But Littré was unable successfully to repair the gaps that he had torn in Comte's philosophy, or to construct a new one of his own. When in the 1870's Darwinian evolutionism became dominant in France, the eclipse of the postivist theory of social development was assured. Littré nevertheless retained and applied till the end of his life the essential and most fruitful elements of the positivist *method*. These were, as has been indicated, an approach to history as a process involving the gradual emancipation of the human mind from theological and metaphysical ideas, the concept of the modern world as a society dominated by scientific thought and industrial pursuits, and lastly, descriptive, factual techniques of social analysis.[10]

In purging positivism of its dross, in retaining only its method, its secular approach to historical phenomena, Littré turned back to the point of departure of nineteenth century

7 "Littré," wrote Caro, "was not an originator of ideas, but when one was presented to him even in a sketchy and unfinished form, he was only too ready to adopt and cling to it as it was, right to the time when he realized that it was, after all, only a partial expression of the truth." "Émile Littré," *op. cit.*, 537.

8 Comte's religious conversion brought about a split in the ranks of his followers everywhere. Some founded positivist churches, others, Littré among them, adhered in some degree to the master's earlier theories.

9 Marin Ferraz, *Socialisme, naturalisme, positivisme* (Paris, 4th ed., n. d.), 417.

10 Littré, *Paroles de philosophie positive* (Paris, 1863), 92 ff.

philosophical thought, to the point where the eighteenth century had left off. The exclusion of theological and metaphysical concepts from social thought, a theory of progress as a form of universal fatality, the application of scientific method to the study of society, these were preeminently contributions of the Enlightenment. The positivist method, as finally adopted by Littré, was little more than a restatement of leading eighteenth century ideas. How this method, applied to nineteenth century conditions, produced a *republican sociology*, will be shown in the sequel.

II

With the coming of the Third Republic Littré's influence as a practical thinker grew even as his theoretical importance waned.[11] His early political opinions had been no less immature than those of most of his republican contemporaries, and his outlook in the middle years of the century had been characterized by a shallow optimism and a flair for making predictions that were ludicrously deflated by the actual course of events.[12] At the time of the February Revolution Littré, under the illusion that the workers were as positivist as himself, declared in favor of a strong central government for France nominated and controlled by the Paris *Sansculottes*.[13] The role of the parliamentary regime based upon universal suffrage should, he considered, be kept to a minimum. In fact, socialism, posi-

11 Littré's ideas were expressed almost exclusively in articles and pamphlets. A chronological listing of his works and of the journals to which he contributed will be found in *Polybiblion, op. cit.* Many of Littré's articles have been collected and published in book form. These collections, of great value for the study of his philosophy and political thought, are: *Conservation, révolution, et positivisme* (1st. and 2nd. editions, Paris 1852 and 1879 respectively) ; *Fragments de philosophie positive et de sociologie contemporaine* (Paris, 1876) ; and *De l'établissement de la Troisième République* (Paris, 1880).

12 In 1850 Littré predicted that the positivist era was at hand and that war, killed by industry, would now forever be banished from Europe. " Paix occidentale," *Le National*, November 18, 1850.

13 " Révision de la Constitution," *ibid.*, October 1, 1849.

tivism, and revolution were to Littré at this time all one and the same thing. After the destruction of *Sansculotte* and Jacobin strength in the conflicts of 1848 and 1849, he raised the banner of socialism in the *National* and campaigned under it until the *coup d'état* of 1851. " Socialism," he wrote " . . . serves us as a flag and cannot, for the moment, serve as anything else. All those who want the revolution to stop or to be rolled back are hostile to socialism. All those who want the revolution to be completed are favorable to it. . . ." [14]

During the Napoleonic era Littré became appalled at what he considered his inconceivable rashness and naiveté. By 1870 it was clear to him that the workers were revolutionaries with ideas and initiative of their own that could in no way be reconciled with positivist aims.[15] His distrust of the Left was further deepened by the experiences of the Paris *Commune* in 1871, an episode in which he professed to find confirmation of his worst fears about the ' violent tendencies ' of the proletariat. From that time on he demonstrated an almost pathological horror of popular movements and uprisings. He insisted that a workers' government could only end either in anarchy or a recrudescence of dictatorship.

Littré thus repudiated his old ideas of direct popular rule. Previously, as we have seen above, he had little use for parliamentary institutions, but after 1870 he began to view them in a new light. The *bourgeois* Republic, clearly, had obvious advantages as a type of *indirect* government by means of which the passions of ' the mob ' could be held in check and the sober middle-classes could effectively rule the country.[16] He embraced this conclusion with characteristic enthusiasm and be-

14 " Socialisme," *ibid.*, August 20, 1849.

15 " Quelque mots de préambule," being the introduction to Felix Aroux' *Ce qu'est le socialisme* (Paris, 1870) ; and the section on " Socialisme " in " De la situation que les derniers événements ont faite à l'Europe, au socialisme et à la France," *Philosophie positive*, VII (1870-1871), 185-194.

16 *Par quelle conduite la République française doit-elle consolider le succès qu'elle a obtenu?* (Paris, 1873), 13 ff.

came from 1871 on an ardent defender of representative institutions based upon universal suffrage.

If such institutions were challenged by the proletariat on the one side, they were no less menaced by royalist reaction on the other. Regardless of his views concerning the royalist parties —and these views, as will be seen later, changed during the seventies—Littré considered that the central strength of the Right lay in the Church, and that the latter was an agency which must be fought because it threatened to delay indefinitely the establishment in France of a firmly based liberal regime. Most of his life Littré showed that hostility to clerical influence and institutions which we have seen to be a traditional characteristic of republican thought. Positivism, which he had spent so long in teaching, was a philosophy whose main attack was directed against theological belief and ecclesiastical organization. Teaching as it did that the whole of human history marked a progress from supernatural ideas and authoritarian rule to the age of science and industry, positivist doctrine was essentially anticlerical. The positivists, in contrast to Renouvier, had respect for the contribution of the Catholic Church to European culture at the height of its power during the Middle Ages; but they stressed, no less emphatically, that the period of the Church's utility to society was long since past. In Littré's own words, " the social role formerly filled by the Church was reaching its end; its influence was becoming a drag upon the development of a new age." [17]

For Littré and the liberals, then, the problem, in the conditions which prevailed in France in 1871, was to establish a parliamentary regime. Anticlerical and anti-socialist, but at the same time rooted as far as possible in tradition and able to compel popular respect, such a regime, he thought, would permit the bourgeoisie to exercize the freedom of action which it wanted for the exploitation of national resources in an industrial age. But in the modern world the institutions of parliamentary democracy have been organized in two types of state-

17 " Le moment actuel," Philosophie positive, X (1873), 439.

form, those of the republic and those of the constitutional
monarchy. Was there any reason why one of these forms should
be preferred to the other?
In dealing with this question [18] Littré turned wistful eyes
to England. There, he considered, the problem had been solved
with great success; since the seventeenth century parliamentary
institutions had been grafted onto an antique social structure
with a minimum of disturbance. Stable government under a
long-established dynasty had been combined with " the claims
of liberty and democracy." But in France a different historical
development made the problem far more complex. The institutions that, traditionally, had made for conservatism and
stability in the state had been swept away by the Great Revolution; since that time the country had never recovered its
balance, but had been a prey to revolution and counter-revolution turn by turn. The problem, in Littré's own words, was
fundamentally how ". . . to remake institutions which will
really strike root and not be at the mercy of military con-
spiracy and of urban disorder."
In the early seventies, then, which form of parliamentary
government could the liberal *bourgeoisie* establish most rapidly
and successfully in France? Which would soonest win the support of the people? Littré considered that the answer could not
long be in doubt. The task of establishing the Republic would
not be an easy one, in the face of opposition from the royalists,
the Church, and from a certain section of the liberal party itself; but it would be infinitely easier than restoring the
monarchy. For this reason the Republic should be preferred.[19]
Littré's republican preference was a cautious one, and expressed with many reservations. At first he considered that
the principle danger came from the Right which, in the form

18 Littré's ideas on the republic as a state-form are expressed in " De la
forme républicaine en France," *Philosophie positive*, VIII (1872), 161 ff.;
" De la durée de la République," *ibid.*, XXIII (1879), 454-465; and " La
composition de la société française et la République," *La Nouvelle Revue*,
II (1880), 481 ff.

19 For an elaboration of this position, see below, 98-99.

of the royalist parties and the Church, was still strongly entrenched in French society; and he warned republicans that
it was foolish to believe that "by means of a word we have
changed the character and the institutions of old France." But
in the late seventies Littré's attitude with respect to the Right
underwent a marked change. After about 1877 he ceased to
regard it as an intransigent menace, but rather as a bulwark
of the established order, upon which republicans should lean
with increasing strength. The reason for this shift in his position was the revival of the labor movement as an organized
political force. With the destruction of the *Commune* in 1871
Littré and the liberal republicans had little to fear from the
Left and its revolutionary aims. But the respite was brief.
Congresses of organized labor were held from 1876 on; collectivist doctrines were canvassed, and finally in 1879 the establishment of a revolutionary socialist party was voted for.
Littré began to fear again for the stability of the liberal regime
and to revise his attitude toward the Right. He came to the
conclusion that the monarchy, given the risk of another civil
war, retained great potential value for France; and thereafter
he advocated the continued toleration on French soil of the
Napoleonic, Bourbon and Orleanist dynasties.[20]

Littré justified his plea on behalf of the royalist enemies of
the Republic by the formulation of his *doctrine des encas*.[21]
If, as he thought possible, the republic might collapse under
the stress of class conflict, conservatives would have ready to
hand "offers of service against the time when the public safety
might be in jeopardy." It was not at all impossible that the
republican regime might itself prove only to have been a temporary expedient, to be in turn discarded:

20 "...in this unprecedented situation the best thing is to let [the
dynasties] alone, provided that their activities are under surveillance...."
"Société française," *op. cit.*, 483.

21 There is no exact English equivalent for *encas*. It denotes anything that
is kept by against an emergency.

" I am an optimist," [he wrote] " but not a blind one, with regard to the duration of the Republic. We must take note of republican conflicts and republican weakness for revolutionary and evilly disposed socialist elements. All this sort of thing troubles the mind, alarms the ' interests,' shakes the stability of the regime and makes one want to run for shelter to the first refuge that offers itself against the disturbers of order. In such a situation the monarchical *encas* would be there." [22]

For these reasons, Littré concluded, it was clearly a good tactic for liberals to preserve the dynasties, keep them on French soil and exploit the advantages which they offered.

Littré in the last resort thus based his republicanism upon expediency. In this, as opposed to Renouvier, he expressed one of the traditional characteristics of Girondism, namely that the choice of the state-form was a matter of comparative indifference so long as the essentials of *bourgeois* domination were secured.

III

With the reservations noted above—and they are significant ones—Littré after 1870 favored the parliamentary republic as the political basis of *bourgeois* rule so long as it could guarantee the social stability necessary for industrial development. For such a regime there was only one sound basis, namely, the consent of the people as expressed through universal suffrage and representative government. Littré, in common with all other republicans, considered this a first principle of political theory.[23] But universal suffrage, in itself, was not enough to consolidate the democratic republic and to guarantee that it would be supported by the masses. The experience of the

22 " Société française," *op. cit.*, 487. This doctrine was stigmatized by François Pillon as ' dreaming of looking for national salvation outside the republic.' *Critique philosophique*, 1883, I, 24.

23 Littré's position on universal suffrage as the basis of the *bourgeois* state was developed in " Le suffrage universel en France," *Philosophie positive*, IV (1869), 31 ff.

Second Republic, and its humiliating defeat at the hands of Louis Napoleon, had been sufficient proof of that. Such a regime could only be consolidated by encouraging, over a period of time, what Littré vaguely referred to as "the full development of social forces," [24] that is, by strengthening the social basis upon which the Republic rested. In elaborating this point, in linking the future of the republican regime with the attitude to it of the various classes in society, Littré evolved, not a clear-cut political theory, but what might best be characterized as a republican *sociology*.

The stability of the Republic, in Littré's view, must depend upon the support of three principal classes. The most important of these, in his opinion, if not the most numerous, was the *bourgeoisie*.[25] The liberalism of the richer members of this class had in the past been monarchical rather than republican; and they had preferred parliamentary institutions based upon a limited, property franchise rather than upon universal manhood suffrage, as, for example, during the first National Assembly of 1789 and during the Orleanist regime of 1830 to 1848. But experience, said Littré, had shown these people that the establishment of constitutional monarchy was not possible in the conditions that existed in France at the end of the nineteenth century. In the first place, the conflicts and the divisions that prevailed among the dynastic parties had prevented them from coming to an agreement among themselves. Failing such agreement a restoration was impossible and the position of the constitutional monarchists was untenable, as had been amply demonstrated by the experience of the years 1871 to 1875.[26] In the second place, the monarchical tradition had been

24 "Le moment actuel," *Philosophie positive*, X (1873), 431.

25 Littré conceived of the *bourgeoisie* as a *bloc*, linked at the top with the old ruling classes and at the bottom with the people. The Jacobins he regarded simply as revolutionaries, evidently failing to identify them with the mass of small property-owners whose interests they usually represented. "Société française," *op. cit.*, 499.

26 The period 1871 to 1875 was characterized by open intrigues among the royalist factions as they strove to compose their differences and to take ad-

destroyed by the French Revolution, and had never since succeeded in regaining its hold over the nation. The republican tradition, on the contrary, had grown and become increasingly strong during the course of the nineteenth century, until, in the 1870's, it had become rooted among the people, particularly the working people.

For these reasons the *bourgeoisie*, said Littré, had understood that the reestablishment of monarchy was impracticable, and they had therefore rallied to the republic. " The republican regime," he pointed out, " guarantees the *bourgeoisie* against counter-revolution, which it fears: if it also provides guarantees against upheavals from the Left, the middle-classes will support it without regret."

Littré's idea that the *theoretical* rule of the people in a republic might be combined with the *actual* rule of a *bourgeois élite* reflected another of the traditional characteristics of Girondism. This *élite,* he considered, was not a closed caste but a group into which the successful and the wealthy might easily graduate. Its nucleus was composed of the remnants of the nobility which the republic inherited from the old regime and from the dynastic nineteenth century.[27] The diverse elements of this liberal aristocracy would be the effective rulers of the Third Republic: from it, thought Littré, the people would choose its parliamentary representatives. " It is obvious," he wrote, " that universal suffrage, by virtue of its peculiar

---

vantage of the opportunity awaiting them to restore the monarchy. Bourbons and Orleanists were both equally opposed to the Bonapartists, but were powerless to come to an agreement among themselves, divided, as they were, by the divergence of the interests and ideas which they represented. For this reason the reestablishment of the monarchy was not practicable.

27 " Whether we like it or not," he wrote, " the Republic will contain a noble class.... Nobles ... maintain a certain elevated level of polite society, good manners, language, courtesy, respect for women, all of which are precious qualities. I have a high respect for these things which democracy, with its roughness and vulgarity, does not favor.... In a democracy it is necessary to reconstitute, not a closed aristocracy, for that is impossible, but an open one, and to borrow from it the correctives which democratic nomination requires." " Société française," *op. cit.,* 490, 491.

character will choose its representatives from that number [i.e., from the *élite*]. Mistakes will be made, that goes without saying, but they will not affect the total result. The Chamber directly, the Senate indirectly, and the President more indirectly still, will represent those aristocratic choices of which I am in favor." [28]

The peasantry was the second and most numerous group in France that would provide a basis for the republican regime. Littré pointed out that the peasantry possessed no abstract or theoretical taste for the Republic, and that twice during the nineteenth century they had in fact embraced Bonapartism as a guarantee against the return of the ecclesiastical and lay nobility and as a measure of security against the radicalism of the towns.[29] Republican policy, then, if it wished to secure peasant support, must continue the Bonapartist tradition of guaranteeing peasant interests against royalism on the one side and against ' confiscatory socialism ' on the other. If this were done, Littré thought, the peasantry would " become a basis of stability very desirable in these times of political uncertainty."

The third social group which must be taken into account in founding the republic was, of course, the proletariat. If France was struggling to shake off the grip of an authoritarian past it had to fight, in Littré's opinion, an equally hard battle against those " revolutionary habits, which, I make bold to say, are no less fatal to the Republic than the machinations

28 Littré did not, of course, exclude from the ranks of the *bourgeois* aristocracy either "eminent workers or socialists with authority." *Par quelle conduite la République française peut-elle consolider le succès qu'elle a obtenu, op. cit.*, 14.

29 Bonapartism had very real and deep roots among the French people, and in particular among the peasants. More a legend than a program, more a piece of crude poetry than a cause, it lived on in the hearts of cultivators many of whom loved the rule of a flesh-and-blood soldier better than a humdrum parliamentary regime whose only function in the past had been, so it seemed, the imposition of heavier and heavier taxes upon small property. The peasants with their long memories still smarted under the effort of the republicans in 1848 to shift the burden of the national debt onto their shoulders.

of the royalists."[30] Littré included both Jacobins and *Sansculottes* in the revolutionary party, and characterized them as "violent, without intelligence, unbelievably ignorant even of the things going on around them. . . ."[31] The workers, whom, after the peasantry, he thought of as "the second great fraction of our people," were essentially revolutionaries; liberalism was little honored among them and less practiced. They were, it is true, the most consistent and devoted of anti-royalists, who had remained true to the republican ideal throughout the nineteenth century and had always been ready to sacrifice themselves for it.[32] But the workers' ideal was not the liberal, but the democratic and socialist Republic; their aims involved the abolition of the *bourgeoisie* and of property, and were hence not only in direct conflict with Girondism but incompatible with its continued existence.

Littré considered that the revolutionary aims of the proletariat could not be realized in France. A minority of the total population, the workers might make themselves temporarily masters of the country, but they could not succeed in the long run in imposing their program, since they would dash themselves in vain against the resistance of the property-owning peasantry and middle-classes. If, however, proletarian aims were not realizable, they were a distinct danger to republican stability, since they produced class conflict and hence could delay indefinitely the establishment of a regime which would have the support of the propertied interests. It must, therefore, be a fundamental part of republican policy to neutralize the proletarian capacity for harm by weaning the workers from revolutionary ideas and by rallying them to the *bourgeois* Republic by means of a policy of 'social conciliation.'[33]

---

30 "Le moment actuel," *op. cit.*, 427.

31 *Ibid.*, 430. Littré considered socialism as merely the left wing of Jacobinism; both he considered used intransigent and doctrinaire tactics, and both were the enemies of liberalism.

32 "These people," he wrote, "are republican by nature, by instinct, and for them the republic is a sort of faith for which they are ready to sacrifice themselves." "Société française," *op. cit.*, 493.

33 For an elaboration of this tactic, see below, 104-105.

If the Republic was challenged by the proletariat on the one side, it was no less menaced by royalist reaction on the other. The danger from the Right, thought Littré, lay in the fact that the defeated royalists might refuse to recognize the regime and might plot to overturn it.[34] As has been seen above Littré, toward the end of the seventies, began to discount the royalist menace, and to stress the potential value to parliamentary institutions of the monarchical *encas*. But this position must not lead us to underestimate the incompatibility of the liberal democratic Republic and the royalist parties. Littré was not disposed to underestimate the danger that the latter would once more plunge the country into civil war and hence indefinitely delay the development of liberal institutions in France. The general contradiction involved in this position of both opposing the Right and regarding it as a potential ally may be said to have sprung from the contradictory position of the liberal *bourgeoisie* itself; to become politically the dominating class it was compelled to face, as it were, in two directions at once, and to fight a double battle, now engaging the forces of the ecclesiastical and dynastic Right, now colliding head-on with the proletarian Left.

The parliamentary Republic, then, was in Littré's eyes a regime which, to endure, must win the confidence of the liberal *bourgeoisie* and of the peasantry, and must hold in check the reactionary influence of the Right on one side and the revolutionary tendencies of Jacobinism on the other.[35] The *tactics* by means of which the liberals planned to achieve these aims, have become known as *parliamentary opportunism*: they have already been touched upon in connection with Renouvier. They consisted chiefly of a plan of national education, a policy of ' social conciliation,' and, ultimately, the disestablishment of the Church. Although Littré and Renouvier were here es-

34 This danger was set forth at length in Littré's *Restauration de la légitimité et de ses alliés* (Paris, 1873).

35 I use the term Jacobinism here in the sense in which Littré understood it, as denoting radicals and socialists indifferently.

sentially in agreement, there were at times substantial differences of emphasis between them: Renouvier stressed the moral element in education, but Littré gave a more clear-sighted exposition of its *rationale*.[36] Education, he explained, must be regarded as a weapon of the liberal state for three reasons. As an instrument of propaganda it would strengthen the hold of the regime upon the people; as scientific and non-sectarian instruction it would strike at the Church and nullify the latter's hold upon the youth; as a means of popular enlightenment it would loosen the hold of socialist doctrine upon the workers and would help them to develop cooperative and mutual aid societies, and hence to follow the narrow path of republican virtue. Littré, further, differed from Renouvier as to the relationship of education and social reform, asserting that education must be introduced *prior* to social reform, and not simultaneously with it. Lay education alone was the key to the establishment of the liberal republic and the solution of its first and most difficult problem. Once introduced social and other problems of the state could be met and solved one by one.

Before the coming of the Third Republic Littré was a consistent advocate of the separation of Church and state. In his last years he reversed himself on this question and not only defended the *Concordat* but also the Church's right to continue its educational activities everywhere except in the elementary schools.[37] This change of position was dictated by expediency; Littré feared that to raise prematurely the issue of disestablishment would reawaken the anticlerical passions of the Left and thus bring once more into question the stability of the regime. It would in addition alienate the Right and make the

36 Littré's influence on republican educational policy was very great indeed. The implications in the educational field of positivist ideas are developed in many places in his writings; they are clearly summed up in Louis Navez, *Éducation et instruction* (Brussels, 1880).

37 Littré first put forward this position in his article " Le catholicisme selon le suffrage universel," *Philosophie positive*, XXIII (1879), 33-46. It caused a sensation at the time, surprising, as Littré himself said, both his friends and his enemies.

republic unpopular with the peasants.[38] He concluded that the abolition of the *budget des cultes* must be postponed to an indefinite future. Clericalism, even as royalism, had its uses as a brake upon the radicals and as a means of conferring a certain respectability upon the conservative Republic. Littré and Renouvier here saw eye to eye as to the desirability of avoiding an open rupture with Catholicism.

A difference of emphasis between Renouvier and Littré was evident in connection with the tactics of ' social concilia-tion.' Littré regarded social reform as subordinate to educa-tional reform, and concerned himself with it little. Socialism, he considered, might be divided into two types, revolutionary and practical.[39] The former, as has been seen, he regarded as incompatible with liberal aims and the liberal republic. The latter he defined as that doctrine " which urges workers to occupy themselves with the improvement of their lot, directs them toward cooperative enterprises, busies itself with un-employment, strikes and the daily struggle with employers." [40] This, in his opinion, was the only legitimate type of social action, and this the workers should be encouraged to take up. They should be urged to raise their demands " on the terrain of the parliamentary republic " where their legitimate needs would certainly be satisfied through discussion and the " firm demonstration of working class desires." To be sure, only a minority of workers, in the first decade of the Republic, were in favor of the type of action which Littré advocated, but this did not dismay him. " To have on one's side a minority," he wrote, " is, of all forces, that most suited to modify the feel-ings and ideas of the majority, which remains, I am convinced, intransigent and revolutionary, but whose intransigence will

38 " ... the republic would once more get itself into serious trouble," he wrote, " if it tried to strike so direct a blow at the traditions, habits, beliefs, of the bulk of the nation." " Société française," *op. cit.*, 500.

39 *Par quelle conduite, op. cit.*, 10, 11.

40 *Loc. cit.* Littré's views on reformist socialism may be found detailed in " Le socialisme," *Philosophie positive*, VII (1870-1871), *op. cit.*

not defend them against the longrun influence of good intentions and measures." [41]

Such, in brief, was the advice which Littré offered to the liberal republicans during the first decade of the Third Republic. Littré's ideas, as we have seen, were set forth at a time when the positivist philosophy upon which those ideas were based was rapidly being supplanted by more advanced types of evolutionary thought; and therefore he founded nothing that could, by any stretch of imagination, be called a philosophical school. Littré's work, nonetheless, found many followers among the liberal and radical republicans. There were, indeed, few neo-Girondists or neo-Jacobins who were not influenced either by the methods of social analysis which he demonstrated or by the republicanism which he advocated.

IV

In 1883, the year following Littré's death, a young scholar from the provinces arrived in Paris. He came to defend a dissertation on French tragedy in the sixteenth century for the degree of Doctor of Letters. This young man, Émile Faguet, who thus announced himself, was to remain for a quarter of a century the single most important exponent of Littré's ideas and the continuator of his method. Faguet, until the turn of the century, was preeminently a literary critic and an historian of French letters. But after 1900, with the publication of a series of works on politics and morals, he established himself as a leading spokesman of liberal republicanism in the period of its decline; and he achieved recognition as a man who was outstanding in the art of applying the positivist method to the study of political problems and to the exposition of political theory.

Faguet's liberal republicanism was a restatement of Littré's theory of the rule of the *bourgeois élite* in a regime of universal suffrage. But between Littré's pen and Faguet's this theory underwent a sharp change. After the turn of the century

41 " Société française," *op. cit.*, 497.

liberal republicanism was no longer dominant in France either as a party or as a creed. It was assailed in particular by the ideas and the forces of the neo-Jacobins and the *Sansculottes*. Faguet's political philosophy reflected this change, where liberal republicanism had shifted from being a dominant creed to one on the defensive. He assumed a sharply hostile attitude to the claims of what he termed the 'democratic,' as opposed to the 'liberal,' republic. Sniping at those institutions of democracy which the neo-Girondists had themselves installed in France, Faguet advocated a return to the system of government by caste, by a closed oligarchy protected by various political devices from the pressures of universal suffrage. The degeneration of the neo-Girondist ideal into a theory of social and political reaction is thus apparent in Faguet's work.

The personal history of Émile Faguet [42] (1847-1916), as one of his biographers has said, "lies almost entirely in the publications that came from his pen." [43] The son of a teacher of classics at Poitiers, Faguet followed his father's profession for the better part of his youth. During the first stormy years of the Republic he was teaching the classics in obscurity at various provincial *lycées*. In 1883, following the completion of his work for the degree of Doctor of Letters, Faguet received his first appointment in the capital at the *lycée* Charlemagne, and embarked forthwith on a career as writer, reviewer and dramatic critic. In 1890 he achieved fame with the

42 One of the best short sketches of Faguet's life, though incomplete, is to be found in Alphonse Séché, *Émile Faguet* (Paris, 1904); see also the summary in *Polybiblion, 2ᵉ série*, LXXXIV (Jul.-Dec. 1916). A. Belis, *Le Critique française à la fin du 19ᵉ siècle* (Paris, 1926), contains a well-written account of Faguet's intellectual evolution. Numerous appraisals of his literary, critical and personal qualities have appeared, many of them ephemeral. The most important are listed in Séché, *op. cit.*, 38, 39. The best of more recent appraisals is Maurice Duval, *Émile Faguet, le critique, le moraliste, le sociologue* (Paris, 1911). See also Henri Bordeaux, *Pèlerinages littéraires* (Paris, 1905), and N. Weiss, "Émile Faguet," *Bulletin historique et littéraire de la société de l'histoire du protestantisme français*, LXII (1913), 150-173.

43 Ernest Seillière, *Émile Faguet* (Paris, 1938), 11.

publication of a book on the Enlightenment,[44] and in the same year began to teach French literature at the Sorbonne. In 1895 he was appointed professor of French poetry there, a position which he held until his death. His literary work received national recognition when he was received into the *Académie Française* in 1901.

Such are the bare facts of a life that was intrinsically remarkable only for its prodigious and sustained literary activity.[45] Faguet, it must be noted, was thirty-five years old before he began to write for the public: his outlook upon the world was mature when he began his creative work, and no perceptible evolution is to be detected in it. But there was over the years an emphatic change in Faguet's intellectual interests and hence in the subject-matter with which he was concerned. At first he wrote as a literary critic and historian of French literature, producing between 1883 and 1890 a series of purely literary studies.[46] But gradually he became absorbed in the study of men whose lives had been devoted to the elaboration of political, moral, and social ideas. The beginning of this new stage in Faguet's interests was marked by the publication in 1891 of the first volume of his famous *Politiques et moralistes du 19ᵉ siècle*. From that time until 1900 Faguet, while in no way ceasing to write works of literary criticism, was more and more concerned with the history of ideas and the examina-

44 *Études littéraires sur le 18ᵉ siècle.*

45 Much of Faguet's published work appeared originally in the form articles for literary journals and reviews, daily papers, etc., and in this his pattern of political activity resembled Littré's. Both men were publicists and commentators rather than original thinkers developing their own independent theoretical activity. There is not in existence, so far as is known to the present writer, any complete and properly classified bibliography of Faguet's writings. General but incomplete listings will be found in Duval, Séché and *Polybiblion, op. cit.* See also Belis, *op. cit.*, 105-178.

46 A list of these works will be found in Séché, *op. cit.*, 35, 36. Explanatory comment on these and other of Faguet's literary productions, but hampered by unnecessary diffuseness, will be found in Seillière, *op. cit.*, *passim.*

tion of the lives, personalities and works of France's greatest thinkers.[47]

The final stage of this evolution of interests was inaugurated when Faguet published his *Questions politiques* in 1899. This book was composed of articles and reviews which addressed themselves directly to leading problems of contemporary political and social theory. From this time until his death sixteen years later Faguet was principally concerned with the political and social philosophy of liberal republicanism, with the *critique* of democracy and of socialism, and with the elaboration of his own views on the nature of the *élite* that should rule in the *bourgeois* republican state.[48]

Faguet's evolution is of importance for the correct understanding and classification of his voluminous work. It has been excellently summarized by the writer who first drew attention to it.

> " Faguet " [wrote Belis] " made his first appearance in the guise of a literary critic. More and more attracted by writers whose specialty was ideas, he became a critic of moralists, philosophers, and systematizers; finally he yielded to his inclinations and devoted himself to the study of those great

47 The second and third volumes of *Politiques et moralistes* were prepared during the nineties and published in 1898 and 1900 respectively.

48 A list of Faguet's writings on contemporary politics is given in Soltau, *French Political Thought, op. cit.*, 303, but it is inadequate, containing both errors and omissions. Faguet's principal works of social and political theory are: *La Patrie* (in the series *Les Dix Commandements*, Paris, n. d.) ; " Sur les idées maitresses de la Révolution," in *L'Œuvre sociale de la Révolution française* (Paris, n.d.) ; *Questions politiques* (articles written in 1898 and 1899, published at Paris, 1899) ; *Problèmes politiques du temps present* (articles written in 1899 and 1900, published at Paris, 1901) ; *L'Anticléricalisme* (Paris, 1906) ; *Le Socialisme en 1907* (Paris, 1907) ; *Discussion politiques* (Paris, 1909) ; *La Démission de la morale* (Paris, 1910) ; *Le Culte de l'incompétence* (Paris, 1910) ; *Et l'horreur des responsabilités* (Paris, 1911) ; *Le Libéralisme* (Paris, 1912). Material of value for the study of Faguet's political outlook is to be found in many other of his works, in particular *Politiques et moralistes, op. cit.*, and *Rousseau penseur* (Paris, 1912).

problems which confront modern society in general and contemporary France in particular." [49]

Faguet lived a retired, academic life. Surrounded by his books and chosen friends he had a marked distaste for the turbulence and passion of everyday existence. His political work might be characterized as a most subtle, intricate and many-sided defense of the existing social order.[50] In this he reflected, like Littré, the aristocratic qualities of neo-Girondism and its profound hostility to the concept of a republic where radical and socialist influences would predominate. Faguet wrote in a direct, conversational style and constantly resorted to dialogue for the purpose of stating, developing and refuting various political positions and points of view. It might in fact be said that he was one of the most skilful dialecticians of the nineteenth century. And yet his dialectic, even as that of his master Plato, was in every sense an esoteric production. Developed with exhaustive detail [51] it demands of the reader the most prolonged and sustained effort of attention. It appealed, and was intended to appeal, to a comparatively limited circle of intellectuals. The latter valued Faguet's elegant and learned formulations because they provided a system of private beliefs rather than a dynamic political doctrine.

The sources of Faguet's inspiration and of his political system were complex, ranging, as has been indicated, from the dialectic of Plato to the positivism of Comte and Littré. Three additional, and major, influences must be mentioned if Faguet's theoretical work is to be fully understood. From Montesquieu and Renan he derived the concept of government by a cultural *élite,* by an aristocracy of the 'best,' most talented people in society, actuated by principles of 'honor' as opposed to self-interest, and ruling quite independently of direct popular pres-

49 Belis, *Critique française, op. cit.,* 109.

50 Victor Giraud, *Écrivains et soldats* (Paris, 1921), 170.

51 Bordeaux described his literary technique as being "as minutely detailed as that of the Dutch masters." *Pèlerinages littéraires, op. cit.,* 83.

sure and control. From Renan, too, he borrowed the idea of a
personal, mystical, freethinking religion which maintained the
Christian moral teaching and tradition while rejecting theological concepts of social evolution and causality. From
Nietzsche, finally, he drew the hostility to democratic ideals
which became a dominant force in his latest writings. Faguet,
in fact, might be characterized as a theorist who valued positivism as a method of social analysis but who wished, at the
same time, to retain Christian virtues as a dike against the
advance of democratic and egalitarian doctrines.[52]

·   ·   ·   ·   ·   ·   ·   ·   ·

Faguet, after Hobbes, traced the origins of social life to the
fact of war. He considered that man's natural bellicosity had
led him to abandon the unbounded freedom of the state of
nature and to seek security in the protection of the political
state. The latter presented itself to him as nothing but the result
of society's need to defend itself against the predatoriness of
the individual. Faguet had no belief in natural, inherent, human
rights, but he adhered notwithstanding to the traditional
Girondist belief that the state should not interfere with man's
initiative and his freedom of action. This signified to him
primarily that the state should not interfere with individual
property rights which, along with Proudhon and Renouvier,
he considered as both the immutable basis of all social life and
the first prerequisite of freedom itself. In his view the state
ought to confine itself to the role of soldier and *gendarme,* on
the one hand maintaining order within a country and on the
other securing national independence through organizing defense against outside attack. Apart from the measures required
to implement these necessary state activities, Faguet considered that the individual should be left completely alone.

52 Bordeaux characterized Faguet as "a Christian positivist with a
penchant for *Renanisme." Pèlerinages littéraires, op. cit.,* 97. Duval made the
same point in describing Faguet as "a positivist who has not ceased to
be a Christian."

Faguet had little to say on the social question that had not already been said by Renouvier, Littré and Secrétan. His views in this case amounted to a reiteration of the desirability of working-class association, in the form of unions and cooperatives, as a panacea for industrial ills.[53] Faguet held the comfortable and emphatic belief that the social question was incapable of a complete solution. In this conviction he fortified himself with the precepts of Christian charity. The poor, he believed, would always be there; all would be well if the wealthy recognized their obligation to relieve suffering by the distribution of alms.

The implications of this position were clearly anti-egalitarian. Earlier neo-Girondist thinkers had recognized this fact but had nonetheless sought to combine an acceptance of social and economic inequality with the advocacy of a strictly egalitarian political theory. Faguet took a further, and quite logical step, in holding that democratic institutions, from their very nature and operation, fostered egalitarian and socialist ideas, and must therefore be abandoned. His criticism of democracy was published in two works that were written in a clear and popular style and that have become the most widely known of his political writings: *The Cult of Incompetence* and *The Dread of Responsibility*.[54] Both works were merely an elaboration of previously published material,[55] but it is in them that we find the clearest and most characteristic exposition of Faguet's anti-democratic views.

In these works Faguet rejected the theory of democracy based upon universal suffrage, and any institutions that were the products of democratic practice. The French parliamentary

53 "... from all points of view, association is the true means and the sole method of emancipating and rehabilitating the proletariat." " Le socialisme en 1899," *Questions politiques, op. cit.*, 230.

54 *Le Culte de l'incompétence, Et l'horreur des responsabilités, op. cit.* Reference is hereafter made to the English editions, New York, 1913 and 1914 respectively.

55 Notably the article " Sur notre régime parlementaire " that appeared in *Problèmes politiques, op. cit.*, 1-91.

regime, he said, was "an apotheosis of incompetence that is well-nigh absolute." [56] But this fact, be it noted, was not linked in his mind with the defects or corruption of those institutions, nor yet with any causes arising out of the poverty and ignorance of the people. Faguet insisted that this incompetence reflected an inadequacy that was inherent in human nature itself. Democracy, he said, and here he quoted Nietzsche with approval, was "a form of decadence." Since the masses in his view distrusted and even hated really aristocratic and talented people, they chose only mediocrities to rule them, men who were as petty and as inept as themselves. He concluded, therefore, that the people were not fit to choose responsible rulers.[57] It followed inescapably that, if this were so, decisions with regard to government must be removed from popular hands. Only in this way might incompetence be avoided and control of the state restored to the hands of the strong, the efficient and the skilled.[58]

A contempt for people and a lack of faith in democracy is apparent in this position. It contrasts markedly with the views on this subject set forth by both Renouvier and Michel. The former on his death-bed expressed disillusionment with the corrupt French *bourgeoisie,* but almost with his last breath affirmed his faith in the people: "hope," he had written, "can only be founded upon the people. By that I mean those who work, peasants, workers, artists, intellectuals. For it is they who constitute, or ought to constitute, a democracy." [59] Michel, too, shortly before his death in 1903, had written in the same vein. "Democracy," he said, "is, in our eyes, not merely something inevitable, but something to be welcomed.

56 *Cult of Incompetence, op. cit.,* 25.

57 *Ibid.,* 29 ff.

58 Faguet explicitly rejected the idea that education might be used as a tool to enlighten and elevate the masses. He referred sneeringly to teachers as "the demagogues of modern democracy," who implant the subversive ideas of popular sovereignty, of egalitarianism. *Ibid.,* 191 ff.

59 *Les Derniers Entretiens, op. cit.,* 97 ff.

We are proud to live in a democracy, and it seems to us that this regime in infinitely superior to any other. . . ." [60] Faguet was voicing, not the calm optimism of the *idéologue,* but the fears and suspicions of the conservative politician. Democracy, to him, challenged liberal republicanism and the continued domination of the *élite.* It was thus synonymous with decadence and must hence be resisted.[61]

Some liberals, who watched with horror the advance of the neo-Jacobins and *Sansculottes* and who wished "to put the brake on democracy," had found a solution in abandoning the Republic and calling openly for the restoration of royalist or authoritarian rule.[62] Proposals of this sort were not acceptable to Faguet, who clearly understood that any attempt to bring back the monarchy would lead to civil war.[63] All that he wished

60 *Doctrine politique de la démocratie, op. cit.,* 28. For Faguet's own view of Michel, see "Un catéchisme démocratique," *Discussions politiques, op. cit.,* 361-421.

61 *Cult of Incompetence, op. cit.,* 222, 226. Mme. Charlotte Muret has, in this connection, pointed out to me that "Faguet was in no sense a politician —purely an intellectual." This is a point which I am not concerned to contest; but it does seem to me significant to stress the conservative political attitude which was the basis of Faguet's intellectual activities.

62 The two most notable intellectuals who took this position were Étienne Vacherot and Arthur Desjardins. Both these men were originally constitutional monarchists who after 1870 aligned themselves with Adolphe Thiers and were prepared to support a liberal Republic. Both with the advance of neo-Jacobinism abandoned this idea and called for the reestablishment of monarchy. Vacherot (1809-1893) was a philosopher, politician and journalist; he wrote many works including *La Démocratie liberale* (Paris, 1892), a kind of political testament that is of great value for the study of the theoretical position of French conservatism at the end of the nineteenth century. Desjardins (1835-1901) was a magistrate, jurist and political theorist. He was advocate-general of the *Cour de Cassation* at Paris from 1875 until his death. The author of numerous works on law, his most important political contribution was *De La Liberté politique dans l'état moderne* (Paris, 1894). Both Vacherot and Desjardins were spokesmen for the idea of the predominance of an aristocratic *élite* in the framework of a monarchical regime.

63 ". . . it would, in my judgment," he wrote, " be an immeasurable misfortune for her (France) to waste her strength in an attempt to restore a monarchy . . . very probably ephemeral, and which if it were not ephemeral would prolong as long as it lasted strife, opposition, civil discord and waste

for—and he wished for it intensely—was a return to the heyday of liberal republicanism, to the fancied serenity of a " Venetian " regime where a republican aristocracy had ruled society undisturbed by those popular pressures and conflicts which were so rapidly transforming the world.[64]

Faguet's aristocratic preferences were expressed, first, in his concept of fundamental law. He regarded law as a most powerful instrument of conservatism and as a brake upon those who wished to depart with undue haste from the traditions of the past. Law, he wrote, constituted a kind of " spiritual aristocracy," enshrining " the rule of those who have lived over those who live, for the benefit of those who shall live hereafter." [65] A truly aristocratic nation, he added, was one that not merely preserved its old aristocracy, but one which " maintains its old legislation inviolate, adding to it reverently and discreetly new laws which combine something of the modern spirit with the spirit of the old." [66] Something of the same mystical reverence for the work of the past as such appeared in Faguet's concept of the nation which, in a fashion reminiscent of Edmund Burke, he regarded as nourished and guided by " traditions faithfully transmitted and religiously shaped." [67] In essence this position represented a blind reliance on the dead hand of the past to bind the hands of the present and to mute the pace of social change.

Faguet, in the second place, wished to bolster his republic against the democratic tide by strengthening the corporative

---

of strength." *The Dread of Responsibility, op. cit.,* 197. *Cf.* also Duval's remark that Faguet remained, not without regret and disillusionment, "a firm and unfaltering republican." *Émile Faguet, op. cit.,* 69.

64 *The Cult of Incompetence* concluded with a plea for the reconciliation of the liberal republicans with their rivals, but under the continued leadership of the former. "The humble," wrote Faguet, "must love their country in loving the great and the great must love their country in loving the humble; and so all classes must be at one...." *Op. cit.,* 236.

65 *Ibid.,* 90.

66 *Loc. cit.*

67 " De l'idée de patrie," *Discours prononcé à la distribution des prix du lycée Janson-de-Sailly,* July 12, 1913 (Paris, 1913), 7.

elements in society. These he defined as aristocratic social entities that had " enough of vitality and of cohesive force and of sense of responsibility to form a group, an association, an assemblage of parts, to organize, to become a living thing, that is to say, a collective person." [68] The most important of such corporations in Faguet's opinion was the Senate. He would have assigned to the upper House, representing not only the popular will but a cultural *élite,* the sovereign political and law-making powers in France. To the lower House, or Chamber of Deputies, composed of the representatives of the people elected by universal suffrage, Faguet would have allowed only the right to veto measures suggested by the Senate.[69] The latter would be aided in ruling the country, he thought, by a number of administrative agencies converted into " entrenched and exclusive corporations." Chief of these would be the magistracy, the army, the clergy, chambers of commerce and labor unions. These corporations would all have one point in common, he considered, in that by the use of various devices of hereditary succession and cooptation they would be removed from popular pressure and the elective principle. In this way the rule of the *élite* could be guaranteed and the people in general maintained in that happy state of political irresponsibility which, according to Faguet, was appropriate for them and which they desired.

Such in brief was Faguet's conception of "a constitutional aristocracy based upon social capacity." With him the ultraconservative implications of the neo-Girondist ideal were developed to a clear and logical conclusion. But by the time that Faguet died these were esoteric doctrines. Neo-Girondism had been replaced in the public mind by more dynamic creeds, to which attention must now be given.

68 *Dread of Responsibility, op. cit.,* 198.

69 "...the representatives of the multitude," he wrote, "are excellent as documents for information, but detestable...as legislators." Popular assemblies, in other words, should be reduced from legislative to consultative bodies. *The Cult of Incompetence, op. cit.,* 28.

PART II
THE THIRD REPUBLIC AND THE NEO-JACOBINS

INTRODUCTORY

THE liberal republicans, it will be remembered, came to power in the political vacuum created by the collapse of the Paris *Commune*. The royalists were discredited by the events of the years 1870 and 1871, and they remained internally disunited. The working class, with its leadership scattered and destroyed, its rank and file demoralized, was deprived of initiative for some years to come. The liberal republicans, accordingly, secured political power with comparative ease. Headed by Gambetta they received a majority at the elections of 1876. In 1877 they engaged in a sharp conflict with the royalist Macmahon, and forced his resignation as president of the Republic. By 1879 they were in control of the executive as well as of the Chamber of Deputies.

Having achieved this victory the liberal republicans hastened to come to terms with the Orleanists and the clericals, whose antagonists they had hitherto been. Under the combined rule of these groups there opened a shameful era of business profiteering, colonial adventures, and political chicane. The regime could evidently be considered a Republic in no more than name. The royalists remained entrenched in local and central administration, in the magistracy, the army, and the Church.[1] Many of them awaited with ill concealed impatience the day when it would again be possible to revive the monarchy.[2]

1 Seignobos gives the following apt summary of the relations between the two dominant social groups. "The conservative party," he says, "found in the administration, the clergy, high finance, big industry and polite society a strength sufficient to offset the exclusively political power of the republican party." The royalists, in other words, occupied key positions in the state, and in social and economic life. The republicans had control merely of the national legislative bodies and of the parliamentary executive. *L'Évolution de la 3ᵉ République, op. cit.*, 56.

2 "With the exception of those that were Protestant or Jewish, almost all the well-to-do families remained hostile to the Republic. It shocked their

It is in the light of this situation that the growth of a so-called 'radical' opposition movement after 1880 among republicans in the Assembly may be explained. The word itself was borrowed from English parliamentary usage.[3] It denoted those who stood for the most thorough-going, the most uncompromising application of liberal republican principles to political and social life.

The radicals charged the liberals with deserting the republican banner and abandoning some of the most important objectives which they had previously championed. In the first place, the accusation went, they had failed to satisfy national aspirations for a democratic state. Almost one hundred years after the Great Revolution France was still burdened with a quasi-royalist regime which inherited from the Second Empire and maintained all sorts of checks upon the development of a political democracy. The radicals charged that by renouncing the struggle against the clericals and royalists the opportunists had given to these groups a freedom of action which they were using to exploit popular discontent with the regime and hence to sweep away the Republic itself.

In the second place, they said, the defection of the opportunists left unsatisfied the people's need for the most elementary social reforms. The radicals were keenly aware of the fact that in the late 'seventies the workers had begun to rebuild their shattered organizations. With the help of *Communards* then returning from exile the labor movement was being rebuilt. Socialist journals were being established, trade unions organized. After 1880 labor began loudly to demand legislation to protect its interests, and the radicals were quick to capitalize upon the political advantage of championing working-class demands. The labor vote, they calculated, would not only give

---

notions of a well-ordered society and threatened the social order to which they were attached by education and the sense of breeding." *Loc. cit.*

3 "... the word dates in France from the July monarchy. Like the rest of parliamentary life, it was an English importation." Thibaudet, *Les Idées politiques, op. cit.*, 119.

them strength in their political battle with the opportunists. It would enable them to combat the revolutionary influences to which the masses were being exposed after 1880 by the rapid growth of Marxist ideology. Republican candidates, particularly in working-class districts, began to stress social as well as political reform; from this circumstance arose the use of the term 'radical-socialist' to denote politicians who were in favor of legislation to promote a minimum of security for the propertyless class.

The formation of a radical parliamentary group was coincidental with the first phase in the parliamentary career of Georges Clemenceau that stretched from 1875 to 1893. Throughout his life Clemenceau was strongly conscious of Jacobin traditions, and this was especially true during his early parliamentary career. When the Republic was endangered by corruption and intrigue he came forward as its defender and carried on a long struggle on behalf of the *bourgeois* regime against the royalists and opportunists. He was convinced at this time—during the period from 1876 to 1893—that the Republic in order to survive must have the cooperation of the workers and that it must, accordingly, make concessions to them as the price of their support. In these years, therefore, he campaigned on the twin issues of republican defense and social reform. From his speeches and writings emerged a radical, neo-Jacobin republican ideal which reflected at least in part the aspirations of the masses and won much influence among them.

In subsequent years Clemenceau jettisoned these early principles and became, above all else, France's spokesman for a war of revenge against Germany. He became a violent advocate of rearmament and urged that all social reform be subordinated to the requirements of war. With his eyes fixed on the coming conflict he did not hesitate to suppress ruthlessly strikes which the workers made in defense of their living standards, nor to repudiate the working-class support for which in earlier years he had made impassioned appeals. And yet, the formulation of Jacobin ideals which Clemenceau made during his early parliamentary career is of considerable importance for the study of republican history and the history of republican theory. The ideas for which he campaigned at this time were, it is true, in no way new. They echoed the century-old concepts of egalitarian democracy championed by Robespierre in 1793 and Ledru-Rollin in 1848. Nevertheless Clemenceau's writing casts considerable light on the specific conditions and problems of the early Third Republic. He tells us why and how the radical movement of those years grew, and what tasks it set for itself. He explains the *raison d'être* of the Radical Party, and from him we can learn the reasons why it supplanted liberal opportunism as the dominant power in the Assembly. He illuminates the relationship at that time of the two classes, the proletariat and the *petite bourgeoisie,* whose interests he considered that the Republic should reflect. Some attention accordingly will be given to his words in the first of the two succeeding chapters.

·   ·   ·   ·   ·   ·   ·   ·   ·

The radical republican group appeared in the Assembly for the first time in 1876. By 1902 this nucleus had blossomed into the Radical and Radical-Socialist Republican Party. Thenceforth it occupied first place numerically in the Chamber of Deputies and exercized a dominating influence over French political life. It constituted the parliamentary expression of what we may, in general, term the *neo-Jacobin* outlook.

In its formative stages, under Clemenceau's leadership, the social basis of neo-Jacobinism was somewhat different from that of neo-Girondism. The latter, as Littré pointed out, represented the position of the well-to-do liberal and industrial *bourgeoisie.* Neo-Jacobinism by contrast, at least in the period from 1876 until the end of the century, expressed the viewpoint of many people much lower in the social and economic scale. It drew support, in the first place, from petty property owners both urban and rural, from the mass of small farmers, shopkeepers and professional people who constituted a large section of the population.[4] It drew support, in the second place, from the proletariat. Historically an important factor in the rise of the Radical Party to power must be sought in the recovery of the labor movement after the *débâcle* of 1871. This gave no small initial impetus to radicalism, but the latter's hold over the labor vote was only a temporary one, and by the beginning of the twentieth century it was no longer significant. Yet, to say that radicalism lost the labor vote is not the same as saying that it lost labor's cooperation. The contrary was in fact the case. Notwithstanding its leaders' declarations of uncompromising hostility to all *bourgeois* groups, labor as organized politically in the unified Socialist Party cooperated in the Assembly with the radicals until well after the outbreak of the first World War.

By 1900 the Radical Party had reached maturity. If, as we have just seen, it had by that time lost the labor vote it received an accession of strength from the liberal republicans themselves. The latter had belatedly come to realize the bankruptcy of *laissez-faire* in the political conditions then prevailing in France, and the need to support a more advanced program as a condition of retaining power. After the turn of the century the Radical Party retained its vast *clientèle* among the *petite bourgeoisie* but was under the actual control of a small group of parliamentary radicals, of liberals turned radical, and of the business interests with which these groups were associated.

Toward the end of the nineteenth century neo-Jacobinism began to diverge not only politically but also philosophically from neo-Girondism. Clemenceau dropped out of politics in 1893. New spokesmen came forward to reconcile Jacobin prin-

4 The radical spokesman Ferdinand Buisson described the radicals as a party of "small farm owners, clerical workers and petty officials." "La politique radicale-socialiste," *La Revue hebdomadaire*, February 1910, 171. Note also Thibaudet's remark that "radical ideology corresponds ... to the average ideas of France in the regions of medium and small property which form the major part of French territory, . . ." *Les Idées politiques, op. cit.,* 170.

ciples with the policies which the Radical Party had been compelled to champion under Clemenceau's guidance.

The problem, in a nutshell, which the theorists were called upon to solve was how to reconcile the traditional liberal theory of *laissez-faire* with a social policy that would permit state intervention in industrial life. Faced with the growing demands of labor for social and factory legislation the opportunists had done nothing but reaffirm the comfortable belief that the workers could emancipate themselves from misery and oppression by organizing mutual aid and cooperative societies. But by the end of the century this position had been attacked and demolished by the socialists, and its inadequacy as a social program was perfectly clear to the working people. It remained for the radicals to define the limits of legislative reform and to bring their political theory into accord with their current practical activity in this direction. The achievement of this task resulted in the formulation of a doctrine that introduced the idea of social reform into neo-Jacobin republican philosophy.

The new doctrine made its appearance shortly before the beginning of the twentieth century under the name of *solidarité*.[5] It immediately won great popularity and was soon adopted as the official philosophy of the Radical Party. It became the mature expression of what I have termed the neo-Jacobin outlook. The imprint of *solidarité* may be seen virtually in the entire program and in many of the measures of the Radical Party from 1901 to 1914.[6]

Solidarité, by contrast with neo-Girondism, was a social rather than a political philosophy. The shift in stress was quite

5 French radical theorists have used the terms *solidarité* and *solidarisme* interchangeably. To find an English equivalent presents real difficulties. 'Solidarity' possesses none of the connotations of its French counterpart, while 'solidarism' has been used in connection with German corporative theory to denote a philosophy of the state which is poles apart from *solidarité*. For this reason only the French term will be used hereafter.

6 During this time radicalism gave itself an official constitution, held annual conferences and became the dominant party in the Republic.

natural in view of the fact that by 1900 the Republic was firmly established and the social question then overshadowed all others in the internal life of the state. It was a reformist, not a revolutionary philosophy, and combated the Marxist thesis that the crisis of modern society could be solved only by the abolition of capitalism and the creation of a collectivist state. It appealed to and justified state intervention as a means for the gradual improvement of the workers' conditions of life. It urged the masses to support a reformist, empirical approach to industrial and social problems, not a revolutionary and collectivist approach. It preached class collaboration and not class conflict. In the hands of the neo-Jacobins *solidarité* was a doctrine that aided substantially in the organization of the Radical Party and in the maintenance of its political supremacy. Its significance for republican thought and for French society at large will engage us in the next chapter but one.

CHAPTER I

GEORGES CLEMENCEAU AND THE RADICAL PARTY

I

SOUTH of the wide Loire at Nantes lies the rolling land of La Vendée. It is a bleak place, scarred with outcroppings of granite and hedged with thickets and walls of stone. In this district Georges Clemenceau was born on September 28, 1841.[1] Here his forebears, petty gentry following the professions of lawyer, doctor, local official, had lived for many generations. Recently the family traditions had been strongly Jacobin; Clemenceau's father had made a veritable cult of the Great Revolution, and he himself recalled in later life that the family home at Aubraie had been cluttered with pictures of Robes-

[1] There is as yet no definitive biography of Clemenceau in any language, though biographical sketches and reminiscences about him are legion. The reader will find a list of the more important works in the excellent bibliography of Geoffrey Bruun's *Clemenceau* (Cambridge, at the Harvard University Press, 1944). Of those in French—and they are a majority—Gustave Geoffroy, *Georges Clemenceau* (Paris, 1919), may be mentioned as a useful outline of the bare facts of the statesman's life, supplemented by a very interesting pictorial collection. The judgments upon Clemenceau made in this book are adulatory and uncritical, and should be treated with reserve. Of the purely political biographies Georges Michon, *Clemenceau* (Paris, 1931), is one of the best and most succinct. It devotes adequate space to Clemenceau's early political career (1876 to 1893) but is weakened by a complete lack of bibliography with respect to primary sources. Of more recent works, that by Pierre Scize (Lyon, 1944) is ephemeral, but a fundamental contribution is, at the moment of writing, awaited from the pen of Alexandre Zévaès.

Of books on Clemenceau in English, Bruun's cited above is by far the most careful and complete that has yet appeared. Others worthy of note are H. M. Hyndman, *Clemenceau* (New York, 1919), and J. Hampden Jackson, *Clemenceau* (London, 1948). Clemenceau's own reminiscences were taken down by his secretary, Jean Martet, shortly before his death. They add much colorful and often valuable detail to the biographical record, and have been published in three volumes, *M. Clemenceau peint par lui-même* and *Le silence de M. Clemenceau* (Paris, 1929) ; and *Le Tigre* (Paris, 1930). *Clemenceau: The Events of his Life as Told by Himself to his Former Secretary, Jean Martet* (New York, 1930) is a one-volume translation of this material.

pierre, St. Just and other great Jacobin heroes.[2] In these traditions Clemenceau was brought up by a father who—if the reminiscences of old age are to be trusted—sought to eradicate by night the conservative ideas of Church and state which the local school teacher implanted by day.[3]

In those days Jacobin opinions could not be held in France without sacrifice, least of all in La Vendée, haunted as it was by memories of a glorious but crumbling royalist past. With the advent of the Second Empire the elder Clemenceau, who practiced medicine at Nantes, became suspect to the imperial authorities and was packed off to exile in Algeria, a fate from which he was saved only by the indignant protest of his fellow-citizens. Through the person of his father Clemenceau was thus at the outset of his career strongly affected both by the Jacobin tradition and by a keen contempt for the Napoleonic regime which negated the republican ideal and heaped indignities upon the family name.

In 1860 Clemenceau went to Paris to study medicine. At this time the Emperor was at the zenith of his power. With the Italian war of 1859 he had launched France into that series of futile and costly adventures which was in the end to bring the country and the dynasty to ruin. Simultaneously the republican movement was reviving. The Paris working people, crushed by the civil war in 1848, were beginning to reorganize their clubs and their unions. Middle-class republicans were beginning to voice their opposition to Louis Napoleon through the press, at public meetings, in the cafés and law-courts. Clemenceau plunged into the growing political ferment of the capital and at once attached himself to one of the numerous republican groups. In 1862 he helped found a literary review, *Le Travail*, which numbered Émile Zola and Jules Méline

2 Martet, *M. Clemenceau peint par lui-même, op. cit.*, 146-7.

3 It may well be believed, as Clemenceau asserts, that head-on collisions occurred in class as a result of this dual education. The irreverent pupil, armed with his father's moral authority, would 'interpellate' the teacher and, as like as not, end by being sent from the room. *Ibid.*, 182.

among its contributors, and was sentenced to a short spell of imprisonment for participating in a republican demonstration. His minor role in the opposition movement came to an end in 1865 when he received his medical degree and set sail for a visit to the United States.

When Clemenceau arrived in America the Civil War was barely over. As a correspondent for the French republican paper *Le Matin* he proceeded to write a series of articles on American politics in which, albeit with many confusions and inconsistencies, he gave vent to firmly Jacobin convictions.[4] Defending the political rights of the Negro people against the Southern plantation owners, Clemenceau expressed his unlimited admiration for the radical republicans whom he considered to be the most consistent champions of Northern democracy and of the emancipated slaves. Indeed, no American statesman after Lincoln's death won his respect as much as Thaddeus Stevens;[5] Clemenceau studied his methods, tactics, and oratorical style with passionate attention, and came to the conclusion that Stevens would remain ". . . with Garrison, Wendell Phillips, Sumner and Lincoln, . . . one of the most interesting figures of the second American Revolution."[6] Clemenceau admired Stevens because he fought uncompromisingly for the extension of democratic rights to the South; and because he had opposed those republicans who, headed by Andrew Johnson, recoiled at the idea of a root-and-branch destruction of the slavocracy, preferring to effect a reconciliation with the latter rather then emancipate the Negro. When in later years Clemenceau too was to lead an onslaught against republicans who had chosen to ally themselves with reaction rather than to attempt its destruction, he recalled the political

4 These articles have been collected and translated in a volume entitled *American Reconstruction* (New York, 1926).

5 To Clemenceau Stevens was a man who had devoted his entire life to the service of a single cause, that is, to the emancipation of the slaves. *American Reconstruction*, 226.

6 *Ibid.*, 227.

analogy and personal models which he had observed in the United States.

With the outbreak of the Franco-Prussian war in 1870 Clemenceau wound up his affairs in America and returned to France. After a brief stay at Nantes he reached Paris in August. All was in confusion; chaos prevailed at the front, where the French troops were being rolled back and bottled up in Sedan. In the capital the officials were paralyzed, the regime was virtually at an end. On September 4 news of the Emperor's capitulation arrived. The people of Paris declared for a republic, and a provisional government was set up. Without much difficulty Clemenceau established official connections and got himself appointed mayor of the working-class district of Montmartre. This post he filled throughout the ensuing four and a half month siege of the capital.

During these months the population suffered severely from cold and privation until an armistice was concluded with the Germans in January 1871. The terms of the agreement provided for the election of a National Assembly with a definite mandate to make peace with Bismarck. In view of the speed with which the elections were conducted and the fact that one-third of French territory was occupied by the enemy, the Assembly was the product of abnormal conditions. Composed largely of royalists, it reflected the desire of the provinces for the speediest possible liquidation of the war upon which Napoleon III had embarked so lightheartedly.

The royalist complexion of this body, sitting at Bordeaux, was a shock to the Parisians, who had conducted their long and bitter resistance in order to defend the Republic, not to restore the monarchy. During the war they had quarreled among themselves as to the type of government and general objectives that should govern the defense of the city. But by February 1871 they had begun to draw together, actuated by a common suspicion of the Assembly's intentions. The National Guard, an army of civilians created at the outset of the war, developed a unified, democratically elected fighting organization and prepared for an emergency.

The royalists, on their side, did nothing to allay the suspicions of the capital. They passed a series of measures which had the effect of further cementing Parisian resistance.[7] February and March witnessed a gradual mounting of the tension. Finally on March 18 Thiers, Chief Executive of the Assembly now installed at Versailles, attempted to disarm Paris by sending in troops to seize the cannon which had been used during the siege. These were now in the possession of the National Guard. Thiers' provocative move ended in failure when the soldiers fraternized with the Paris people and shot two generals, one of whom had ordered them to fire upon the crowd. Thiers and other members of the Versailles government who were at the time in Paris at once fled. The National Guard, at first stupefied to find itself in undisputed control of the city, organized a municipal government—the famous Paris *Commune*— after an interregnum of six days. The *Commune* itself lasted no longer than six weeks, a period during which it flirted with various revolutionary tactics and ideas, but failed to mobilize either its own forces or those of the country at large against Thiers and the royalists. It met its end at the hands of French troops released by Bismarck for the express purpose of putting an end to *Communard* resistance. The *Commune* went down amid the flames of a burning city and scenes of pitiless slaughter.

In March 1871 when war between Paris and Versailles was threatening, Clemenceau and the other mayors of the city attempted to act as go-betweens and to secure a compromise. The resulting negotiations were encouraged by Thiers because they gave him time to group his forces for the expected conflict. Temporizing thus played into the hands of the royalists. His tactics merely earned for Clemenceau the hatred of the

7 Notably the laws on overdue bills and house-rents, the suppression of radical journals, the sentences of death against Flourens and Blanqui, and the appointment of extreme reactionaires like Valentin and Vinoy to positions of power in Paris.

Parisians and the contempt of the Versaillese.[8] He retired to his father's home and returned to Paris only when the civil war was over.

The destruction of the *Commune* was followed by a reign of terror that lasted until 1875. Its supporters were proscribed, its leaders murdered or exiled. During the period of extreme reaction, from 1871 to 1875, Clemenceau busied himself with municipal politics and in the latter year was elected president of the Paris Municipal Council. In the middle seventies the republican movement throughout the country was reviving, and in 1876 Clemenceau was elected as member for the working-class district of Clignancourt. In May he delivered the first of many speeches before the Chamber, choosing as his topic the question of amnesty for the thousands of *Communards* who had been deported or imprisoned. This speech was drawn up with a lawyer's skill and a historian's mastery of detail. Clemenceau very soon became known as a brilliant speaker and as the acknowledged leader of the still small group of radical republicans in the Chamber.

Clemenceau's group remained an insignificant minority within the republican party until 1879, when it broke away from the parent body. When Clemenceau entered the Assembly in 1876 all republicans were united by the desire for victory over the royalists. In that year, as a result of growing republican sentiment throughout France, they secured an electoral victory which enabled them to challenge the political supremacy of the Right. By 1879 they had wrested control of the government from the hands of the by now thoroughly discomfited opposition comprising the coalesced forces of the Orleanists, Bourbons and Bonapartists. But with the victory won the liberal republicans hesitated to push ahead with the reforms which they had previously promised at the polls.[9] They became

8 P. O. Lissagaray, *Histoire de la Commune de 1871* (Paris, 1944), 130, 137 ff., and Edmond Lepelletier, *Histoire de la Commune de 1871* (Paris, 1911), I, 468 ff.

9 The republicans went to the country in 1876 with much the same program as in 1869. See above, 49.

frightened at the resurrection of the socialist movement in the late seventies and sought political stability in an alliance with the very interests which they had previously opposed and which now began to rally to the support of the republican regime.[10]

The situation created by the *volte-face* of the opportunists was unacceptable to Clemenceau. It meant that the Republic was to be a plaything in the hands of the monopolists and financiers.[11] In 1879 he broke with the majority and led a small group of radicals into opposition. The decision was announced with a clap of oratorical thunder in the first of a series of reports which Clemenceau delivered to his electors at the Fernando Circus.[12] He summoned the republicans to proceed at once to carry out their declared program; principally, to clean out the royalists and clericals from the administration, where they were entrenched, and to replace Napoleon III's dictatorial laws by new democratic ones.[13] He followed this blast by again raising the question of amnesty, this time even more sharply than before, and by founding *La Justice* as an organ of daily combat against the moderates.

By these acts the Radical Party was, in effect, brought into being.[14] As its head Clemenceau continued his campaign against the opportunists throughout the eighties. In the elec-

10 " The opportunist majority accepted what remained of the *ancien regime* and wished to live in peace with the powers of the past, the old noble families, the clergy, high finance. These powers they hoped to rally to the Republic." Seignobos, *op. cit.*, 109.

11 *Débats parlementaires (Chambre des Députés)*, 1884, I, 255 ff.

12 A report of this speech, somewhat condensed, will be found in *La République française*, May 13, 1879.

13 Clemenceau had in mind particularly the abolition of the old laws against freedom of speech and meeting, against trade unions, against the *Communards* and the International; and the passage of new laws establishing a secular education system and a unicameral Chamber.

14 Clemenceau and his group "constituted the first nucleus of a radical party oriented along lines laid down in their organ *La Justice*." Ferdinand Buisson, *La Politique radicale*, vol. V of *Collection des doctrines politiques*, ed. A. Mater (Paris, 1908), 66.

tions of 1881 and 1885 the pressure of the small but vociferous radical group was a factor of no small importance in determining the issues upon which the campaigns were fought. In 1881, for example, the opportunists were compelled to declare themselves in favor of constitutional revision, legalization of trade unions and separation of Church and state. Radical pressure, again, played its part in securing passage of republican laws such as the press and public assembly laws of 1881 and the education law of 1882.[15] By 1885 Clemenceau had won a reputation as an outstanding champion of the Republic and of the rights of the people.[16] The radical group held the balance of power in the Chamber of Deputies, and thanks to this fact and his own great popular prestige Clemenceau exerted great personal influence. Not infrequently he dictated the selection of ministers and decided the fate of cabinets, thus enjoying the combination of power and irresponsibility of which he had previously accused his rival Gambetta.[17]

After 1885 Clemenceau encountered increasing difficulty in developing his anti-opportunist movement and in retaining the undivided support of labor. At that time, to be sure, the majority of French workers were still unorganized, they had as yet succeeded in building neither a strong trade-union movement nor a unified political party of their own. But several socialist groups had come into existence which sharply challenged Clemenceau's position as the most ' advanced ' of re-

15 The press law of January and the public assembly law of June 1881 swept away the checks on freedom of press and meeting which had been imposed under the Empire and retained by the Orleanists and opportunists during the first decade of the Republic. Henceforth public meetings might be held without previous authorization and the right to print and retail books and newspapers was open to all. These laws represented a victory for the radical pre-election campaign in the years 1880 and 1881.

16 Alexandre Zévaès, *Jules Guesde* (Paris, 1928), 48, 49.

17 Clemenceau realized that if he accepted power he would be to a large extent a prisoner of the conservatives, and that, as far as his popular reputation was concerned, an hour of office would destroy the effect of years of opposition. Jean Mordacq, *Clemenceau* (Paris, 1939), 8.

publicans, and demolished his claim to be the political spokesman for the working class. Jules Guesde and Paul Lafargue,
the leaders of the *Parti ouvrier français,* carried on a vigorous
polemic against Clemenceau in the socialist press and from innumerable platforms.[18] In years of ceaseless propaganda they
taught workers to accept Marxist, collectivist ideals. These
of course Clemenceau as a Jacobin fiercely repudiated.[19] It was
symptomatic of the change that had occurred when in 1885 he
abandoned the working-class district in Paris which he had
hitherto represented and transferred his constituency to the
rural community of Draguignan in the Var.

Another important factor in weakening Clemenceau's position was the Boulangist movement. By 1885 economic crisis
had become acute and the masses had become disillusioned with
the opportunist regime. Under these conditions the Right was
able with comparative ease to exploit the popular discontent
with the aim of discrediting the Republic and installing a dictatorship. Clemenceau himself contributed to this movement
when in 1886 he thrust his nominee Boulanger, "the republican general," into Freycinet's cabinet as minister for war.
Boulanger rapidly shook off the control of his radical sponsor
and headed for a career of unbridled demagogy, attacking republican institutions and inflaming anti-German feeling among
the masses. His movement was financed by the monarchists,[20]

18 "The efforts of the collectivists," as Weill correctly notes, "were
principally directed against the Radical Party." *Histoire du mouvement social
en France* (Paris, 1924), 237. See in particular *Égalité,* April 14, 21, 28,
May 5, 23 to 26, June 9, Nov. 2, 1880; and the debate against Tony Revillon,
December 18, 1881.

19 "You will never get me," he said with a sneer, "to enter the barracks
and the monasteries which you socialists are preparing for us." *Discours
de M. Clemenceau: compte-rendu de son mandat, Cirque Fernando,* April 11,
1880. Paul Lafargue answered Clemenceau's taunt in a series of articles
"Les couvents et les casernes," that began to appear in *Égalité,* April 28,
1880, and which constitute one of the most brilliant polemics in the history
of French socialist literature.

20 "The money came from the royalists, three million francs from the
Count of Paris, and as much again from the Duchess d'Uzès, heiress of the
wealthiest wine-master of Champagne." Seignobos, *op. cit.,* 137.

but it drew much support from the *petite bourgeoisie* and from a section of the workers. So successful was it in this respect that the left-wing republican movement was thrown back on the defensive for four years.

Boulangism split and severely weakened the radicals. Soon after the movement collapsed in 1889 Clemenceau himself was driven out of politics when his connection with Cornelius Herz was revealed. Herz, a shady financier and company-promoter deeply involved in the Panama affair, was found to have held a controlling interest in *La Justice* ever since 1880.[21] Clemenceau was discredited, beaten at the elections of 1893, and driven into retirement.

II

Clemenceau spent the next nine years in seclusion, earning his living as a journalist and writer of *belles lettres*. His retirement was only interrupted by the Dreyfus affair, in which he appeared as one of the leaders of the revisionist, or pro-Dreyfus coalition.[22] The Dreyfus crisis marked the end of the opportunists as the strongest parliamentary group. After the elections of 1902 this position was assumed by the now powerful Radical Party, and conditions hence arose that favored Clemenceau's return to political life. He was elected Senator for the Var in 1902, an event which inaugurated the second major phase of his public career. As was to be expected, it was not long before he received cabinet rank. In 1906 he became Minister of the Interior in the stopgap Sarrien cabinet. In October of the same year an all-radical ministry was formed under his leadership which lasted for nearly three years and was one of the longest-lived of all governments of the Third Republic.

21 For estimates of the sums of money which passed between Herz and Clemenceau see Bruun, *op. cit.*, 48.

22 Clemenceau's articles on "the affair" have been collected and published in seven volumes totalling over six hundred separate pieces.

The prospects for the Clemenceau ministry might have appeared excellent to a casual observer. The anti-Dreyfus coalition of royalists, nationalists and anti-Semites, already weakened in the elections of 1902, suffered further defeats in those of May 1906. The Radical and Radical-Socialist Party had been returned to the Assembly with nearly fifty per cent of the seats in the Chamber of Deputies, almost enough to govern without the aid of any other group. On assuming the premiership Clemenceau took a step that appeared in conformity with his own past reputation and the election promises of his supporters. He created a special Ministry of Labor under Viviani and announced a grandiose plan of social reforms that included the eight-hour day, workers' pensions, the abolition of the trade-union law of 1884,[23] and the introduction of a progressive income tax.

Notwithstanding these fine promises, there was scarcely a ministry in all the annals of the Third Republic so barren of achievement as this, nor one with so black a record in the use of force to break strikes and smash unions. While the people's representatives were quietly voting themselves an annual pay increase of f.6,000[24] Clemenceau was using troops to smash wage struggles with violence and loss of life.[25] Unabashed parliamentary self-seeking, cynical indifference to the

23 This law made legitimate the organization of trade unions, but it contained certain very undesirable features. Unions were required to register their membership lists with the Prefect, a provision which facilitated blacklisting.

24 This action " produced between the electorate and their representatives a degree of ill-feeling which the conservatives had been unable to create in a quarter of a century's agitation." Seignobos, op. cit., 256.

25 The strike movement of the workers intensified after 1900 owing to a general rise in the price level and a consequent deterioration of the already low living standards of the people. In March 1906 Clemenceau sent in troops to break a mining strike in the Pas-de-Calais, and he arrested the leaders of the Conféderation générale du travail when a sympathy strike was planned. In 1907 he smashed a strike of wine-growers in the South, again using troops and provoking violence at Narbonne. In 1908 he forcibly suppressed a strike of building workers at Villeneuve-Saint-Georges.

interests of the working people, such undeniably was the record of Clemenceau's first ministry. It was clear that a decisive change had taken place in his political orientation.[26] The erstwhile champion of labor and of the progressive republican cause was henceforth to be identified with the most reactionary forces in France. He gave evidence increasingly of autocratic and domineering personal qualities, of a ruthless antagonism toward the Left, which was to find fitting scope in the war dictatorship of 1917 to 1919.

So drastic a political change requires explanation, but it should not distract our attention from Clemenceau's work in the years 1876 to 1893 nor should it blind us to the significance of the ideas which he elaborated during that period. They are of importance from many points of view. In particular they reveal the political and social bases of neo-Jacobinism and provide a key for understanding its subsequent evolution in both the intellectual and parliamentary history of the Third Republic. Before examining these ideas in detail some effort must be made to explain Clemenceau's later repudiation of them.

Ever since 1870, in the first place, Clemenceau was actuated by a passion for revenge against Bismarck's Germany.[27] At the time of the annexation of Alsace-Lorraine in 1871, an event which made a deep impression upon him, Clemenceau decided that it must thenceforth be his mission to arouse the French people from the " cruel indifference " into which their everyday occupations thrust them and to reawaken in them the thirst for " inevitable revenge." [28]

Clemenceau's hatred of Germany was nowhere more clearly illustrated than in his struggle against French colonialism during the eighties. Bismarck, in order to deflect attention from

26 This has been noted by Julius W. Pratt, " Clemenceau and Gambetta, a study in Political Philosophy," *The South Atlantic Quarterly*, XX (1921), 95-104. But the author fails to give an adequate explanation of the change.

27 Jean Ajalbert, *Clemenceau* (Lagny, 1931), 19, 20.

28 See Clemenceau's remarks as related by Camille Ducray, *Clemenceau* (Paris, 1918), 45.

Alsace, encouraged the opportunists to 'compensate' them-selves for its loss by means of colonial acquisitions. He cal-culated—correctly, as it turned out—that this policy would bring French and English interests into collision. This would in turn, he hoped, make the opportunists dependent upon Ger-many for diplomatic support and thus blunt the edge of anti-German resentment in France. It was, therefore, with German acquiescence that the opportunists plunged into overseas ex-pansion first in Tunisia and then in the Far East.

These adventures involved enormous outlays of men and money and were highly unpopular with the French people.[29] Clemenceau subjected them to attack, and in 1882 began an onslaught upon colonialism which reached its peak with the Tonkin *débâcle* of 1885 and the resignation of Jules Ferry. His opposition, it may be noted, was not based upon an ob-jection, as a matter of principle, to land grabbing and the enslavement of foreign peoples. He opposed colonialism only because it diverted French resources and diplomacy from the main target, which in his mind was preparation for the coming war against Germany:

> For us [said he] there is only one possible policy, a policy of revenge. Bismarck has tried to put us off the scent with colonies, which are a frightful waste of effort, men and money, in order to set us at the right moment at loggerheads with England and leave him the *tertius gaudens* [i.e., the third party who draws an advantage from playing the first two off against each other]. . . . It is still, and always will be, to the eastern frontier that we should look.[30]

Clemenceau's advocacy of revenge and *rapprochement* with England put him almost in a class by himself among the leaders

29 Ferry's colonial policies unbalanced the budget, failed to provide promised overseas markets, and ruined the health of the conscripts as a result of wounds and disease acquired in a war of tropical conquest. Seignobos, *op. cit.*, 110.

30 Léon Daudet, *Clemenceau* (English edition, London, 1940), 32.

of the Republic before 1900. Bismarck saw in him an implac-
able foe dominating the French political scene and working
toward his goal with a cold, unrelenting fury at which the
Iron Chancellor had cause to tremble. He was fully aware that,
though Clemenceau was not yet in power and was indeed far
from having a majority in the Chamber, the outbreak of war
would bring him into office.[31]

In 1893, when Clemenceau was swept out of political life,
he was still far from achieving his goal. But when he assumed
power in 1906 profound changes had taken place in the international situation. Bismarck's system had completely broken
down and Europe had become divided into two armed camps.
The prospect of the long-envisaged war of revenge was no
longer a dream but a terrible reality. By 1906 diplomatic and
military preparation for the coming conflict made up virtually
the sum total of Clemenceau's political wisdom. Social reform
no longer played a serious part in his reckoning.[32]

The change in Clemenceau's political orientation was determined, in the second place, by the sharpening of class an-
tagonisms within France. By 1906 the time was long past
when the Radical Party could aspire to that leadership of the
working class, which, as we have seen, it exercized temporarily
in the earlier years of the Republic. The workers had produced
political organizations and leadership of their own. The rising
wave of strikes after 1900 testified to their militancy. Their
leaders repeatedly declared that the outbreak of war would be
a crime which it would be the duty of the workers to oppose.
Clemenceau—as he himself said—was now on the other side
of the barricades. To socialism, strikes, and demonstrations for
peace he presented a fierce opposition.

31 See the comment of the journalist Maurice Szeps, who was personally
acquainted with both Clemenceau and Bismarck, in B. Szeps Zuckerkandl,
Clemenceau tel que je l'ai connu (Alger, 1944), 85, 86.

32 " To profess zeal for social reform was in the spirit of the time but
such zeal must not lead to crushing taxation or collectivist experiments, it
must stop short with token reforms." Bruun, *op. cit.*, 78.

If the responsibility for the first World War is ever finally assessed Clemenceau, no doubt, will come in for some share of the blame. In 1907 he permitted Basil Zaharoff, the international arms king, to establish himself in France and to begin a campaign for rearmament. In the years 1909 to 1914 Clemenceau added his own voice to the clamor for guns and war.[33] When war itself broke out it was at first supported by a majority of the French people, but after three years of slaughter resistance began to mount in the armed forces and on the Left. At this point Clemenceau became of particular value to those who wished to carry on the struggle. The embodiment of *la guerre à outrance*, he still retained much of his old reputation as a great republican leader despite his anti-labor policies of the past decade. In 1917 he was elevated to the position of war dictator with the support of those conservative groups to which in his earlier years he had been bitterly opposed.[34] They were confident that he would carry the struggle to a Carthaginian conclusion and simultaneously crush the resistance of the Left.[35]

With the end of the war in 1919 Clemenceau went into retirement. He died in 1929 after a lifetime in active politics that had spanned nearly the entire era of the Third Republic.

III

Some of the ideas of the radical republicans, in the period 1876 to 1893, were part of the common heritage of all republi-

33 *Ibid.*, 113.

34 " He was elected to make war ... he made it with the aid of any and all groups which would support his policies, the wealthy, the bondholders, the profiteers, the munition makers, with nationalists of the *Action française*, with militarists, with clericals, with a million public officials who feared the new broom of a Socialist administration." Bruun, *op. cit.*, 131. It would be quoting this passage out of context not to point out that Clemenceau, in Bruun's opinion, also made war with the support of " the vast mass of the French people." I raise this point in order to stress that by 1917 Clemenceau had moved far indeed from the Socialist opposition which previously he had championed.

35 *Loc. cit.*

can factions. Clemenceau reemphasized them when the opportunists were either discarding or allowing them to be pushed into the background.[36]

Prominent among these was the concept of the Republic as a lay state. Clemenceau contended that the republican form of government could never be secure so long as Church and state remained officially combined and as long as clerical influences remained dominant in the community. In 1875 he predicted that the conflict between republicans and Catholics over this great issue would dominate the internal history of France during the closing years of the nineteenth century.[37] The necessity of carrying through this struggle appeared to him to be self-evident. The lay state, he said, was established originally by the Revolution, but without lasting success. It had been overturned and kept submerged by successive waves of royalist and clerical reaction. Anticlericalism was therefore an essential part of the republican outlook. It sprang from the necessity of finishing the task which previous generations had been unable to carry through. This was, in a nutshell, to drive the Church out of politics.[38] The principle that the functions of the state, including education, should be entirely free from clerical in-

36 The public speeches and parliamentary addresses which Clemenceau made during the period 1876 to 1893 constitute one of the principal sources for the study of the formation of the Radical Party and its neo-Jacobin concepts. These orations have not yet been published in book form. The historian who will select, edit and annotate this material would doubtless make a useful contribution to the history of the Third Republic. Clemenceau's public speeches were reported *in extenso* in *La Justice*, while the parliamentary addresses are, of course, available in the *Journal officiel*. A complete list of all Clemenceau's speeches for the period 1870 to 1909, together with date of publication in the organ concerned and a brief digest of the contents, has been prepared by Mme. O. Monod, secretary of the *Société des amis de Clemenceau*. It is available at the *Musée Clemenceau* in Paris. A list of the most important of these addresses and other information about them will be found in the bibliography.

37 Presidential speech to the Paris Municipal Council, November 29, 1875.

38 *Journal officiel* (*Chambre des Députés*), 1879, 11221. Speech on amnesty for the *Communards*.

terference, Clemenceau characterized as *the very kernel of republican doctrine.*[39]

Clemenceau directed his attack against the special privileges which the Church enjoyed and upon which its influence was partly based. He pointed out that the principal of these was financial. In the days before separation from the state, the Church maintained its position as the official religion at the expense of the taxpayer. " What is the Church," he said, " if not a huge association living at the expense of those who do not subscribe to its beliefs? " [40] The radicals demanded an end to this regime of financial privilege.[41]

Clemenceau pointed out that the right of association [42] itself, during the early years of the Republic, was an extremely valuable privilege. The working class in particular was discriminated against in that the formation of trade unions was specifically forbidden by law and had in fact been a penal offense ever since the days of the Great Revolution. The Church, by contrast, had enjoyed ever since the conclusion of the *Concordat* virtually complete freedom to organize congregations and religious orders. This privilege was a source of great strength in carrying on propaganda for the royalist and Catholic cause. The republicans were hamstrung by law in their effort to organize and fight back. Responsibility for this state of affairs, Clemenceau added, must be laid at the door of the opportunists, who had left " the enemies of the Republic in

39 *Discours de M. Clemenceau: compte-rendu de son mandat. Cirque Fernando,* April 11, 1880.

40 *Ibid.*

41 In the eighties Clemenceau took the position that taxation for the *budget des cultes* rendered impossible adequate outlays on education and other social services. *Débats parlementaires (Chambre des Députés),* 1884, I, 2496. Speech on the social question.

42 The right of association as used here is not to be confused with the right of assembly or meeting. It denotes the right to form permanent organizations with the power to carry on legal proceedings and to administer property.

possession of this fundamental freedom while denying it to republicans." [43]

Clemenceau thus stood for abolishing the special privileges of the Church. But by this he did not mean that the Republic should embark on a campaign of religious persecution, and on this point he was quite explicit. "The state," he said, "can and must find a place for the Catholic religion, to which it owes the same freedom as to the other cults and forms of opinion." [44] The clerical peril in his view arose not from religion *per se* but from the unnatural union of "two forces that are unlike and antagonistic, the Church and lay society. . . ." These two must be pried apart, by force if necessary, and the right of association must be extended to all republicans, and in particular to the working class. [45]

Clemenceau held that no republican could offer any theoretical objection to the position that he took. He reserved the sharpest point of his attack for the opportunists precisely because they had sacrificed their principles to expediency and jeopardized the Republic through fear for their own immediate class interests. The opportunists, he said, "tremble at the thought of what may happen to themselves and their regime when the protective shield of the monarchy and the clericals has been torn away." [46] For this reason they made an alliance with the royalists at the expense of the Republic. But the principle of the lay state which Clemenceau voiced remained one of the main tenets of neo-Jacobin philosophy. It was to find expression in the laws of 1901 to 1905 that ended the concordatory regime and all but eliminated clerical influence in the schools.

The conflict between radicals and opportunists involved more than a mere tactical controversy on the issue of whether

43 *Cirque Fernando, op. cit.*

44 *Ibid.*

45 *Ibid.*

46 *Discours de M. Clemenceau: à Marseilles, Théâtre des Nations,* October 28, 1880.

or not to join battle with the Church. The two groups disagreed fundamentally on the question of the constitution, and this provided a second major element in Clemenceau's campaign during the early eighties.

The Third Republic had received its legal establishment in 1875. The so-called " constitution " of that year was composed of three separate and distinct laws limiting themselves to the most business-like statement of the powers and functions of the component parts of the State machine; and it was declared that these measures could not be revised or repealed except by means of a special and unusual parliamentary process. These three laws, combined with certain " organic " laws that dealt with the method of election of the National Assembly, established the central political machinery of the Republic.

The main characteristics of this constitution were simple enough: the chief of state, a politically irresponsible president roughly similar to the king of England in power and attributes, was elected by the National Assembly. The Assembly itself was composed of two Houses, one of which was elected by universal manhood suffrage, the other by means of a complex indirect system designed to produce a stable and conservative *bloc* of Senators. The executive proper was composed of a cabinet of ministers chosen from the ranks of either House, and collectively responsible to the Assembly.

The constitution of 1875 was the result of a compromise between the Orleanists and the liberal republicans. The former, setting aside for the moment the thorny question of the royal personage who would preside over the state, were in favor of an Assembly of two Houses chosen on the basis of hereditary and property qualifications. The liberal republicans, by contrast, had a distaste for second Chambers, and were in favor of a single-House Assembly elected by universal suffrage. For a compromise to be arranged between these divergent viewpoints, the liberal republicans had to abandon their objection to an upper House, and the Orleanists had to overcome their repugnance for the principle of universal suffrage. In the light of the menace of Bonapartism, which would again threaten the country if a constitutional settlement were not achieved, the necessary compromise was readily arrived at. It was maintained with the greater ease in that the objection of the liberals to second Chambers had become by the end of the seventies a purely theoretical one. As a matter of practical politics the opportunists understood readily enough that the Senate would constitute an excellent brake upon the operations of universal suffrage as manifested in the Lower House. For this reason when they won a parliamentary majority in 1876 they made no move to revise the compromise which they had made with the Orleanists.

The conservative solution of the state question was anathema to the radicals who considered themselves the leaders of the popular movement and rightly saw that the second Chamber was an instrument for imposing checks upon progressive legislation. Basing themselves upon precedent established in the Great Revolution and in 1848, they raised the demand for a single-House Assembly. Legal sovereignty, they thought, should belong to this body alone. It would express the will of the people directly, unimpeded by the veto or the delaying tactics of a conservative Senate.

Clemenceau accordingly considered that the fight against the constitution of 1875 was a crucial part of the radical agitation for a democratic republic. He attacked the Senate [47] as the leading ' citadel of reaction ' in a campaign that lasted from 1880 to 1885.

One of Clemenceau's main arguments was that the existence of the Senate made much harder the prospects of peaceful social evolution. Most Senators were elected for a period of nine

47 Clemenceau attacked the Presidency too, with its theoretical powers of dissolution of the Chamber of Deputies, powers which he considered to be incompatible with the full sovereignty of a democratic national Assembly. But this position must be considered as secondary to the main onslaught upon the Senate.

years,[48] and they possessed neither political mandate nor responsibility. Their power to block or delay republican legislation was great. He cited as an example the bill to legalize trade unions which prior to its passage in 1884 was debated by both Houses over a period of many months. He pointed out that the Chamber of Deputies agreed in 1882 upon a measure which was not perfect, but was nonetheless a considerable step toward granting labor's demand for full freedom of association. And what happened?

> The Senate [he reported] hastened to adopt a law that nullified all the liberal provisions of the Deputies' bill. A deputy who had failed to have the Chamber adopt his reactionary amendments . . . had himself elected a Senator, was given charge of the bill, and then had the Senate adopt all the provisions which the Chamber had rejected. [general mirth.][49]

Incidents such as these, he claimed, illustrated the anti-democratic role of the Senate. The latter, he said, had been established in 1875 with the specific purpose of

> . . . damming up universal suffrage and raising an insuperable barrier to the will of the nation as legally manifested. This was only the logical continuation of the struggle which the monarchy and its aristocratic or *bourgeois* oligarchies had carried on against the people since the time of the Revolution. . . .[50]

It was, he said, a traditional republican principle that the popular will should be expressed by a properly elected unicameral

48 One-third of the Senate was renewable every three years, a provision which meant that the total period of office for the individual Senator was nine years. A small number—*les inamovibles*—were appointed for life.

49 *Discours de M. Clemenceau: à Lille*, May 20, 1883. The Senate, for example, wrote in an amendment requiring that the names of all union members be recorded with the Prefect. This of course facilitated blacklisting.

50 *Ibid.*

assembly. This principle had been chased out of the Republic by its royalist enemies. It was the task of the radicals to restore it by a revision of the constitution of 1875.[51]

Clemenceau first carried on his revisionist agitation during the election campaign of 1881. He was successful in compelling the liberal republicans to pledge themselves to constitutional reform, but nothing was done until 1884. The liberals then with considerable reluctance decided to call a constitutional convention in view of the necessity of mending their fences for the elections of 1885. The Senate had no desire to revise itself out of existence and refused to consider the idea of the projected Versailles Assembly. Its cooperation was only secured by a government promise that discussion would be confined to purely minor constitutional changes that had been agreed upon beforehand.[52] In 1885, therefore, the radicals again went to the polls with the demand for revision. In the elections they increased their representation in the Assembly, but the campaign was abruptly checked by the rise of the Boulangist movement. Boulanger used the catchword of constitutional reform to win support for a dictatorship thinly veiled as a ' National Republic.' When Clemenceau returned to political life in 1903 it was as a Senator in the upper House which he had previously attacked with such violence. The abandonment of his revisionist ideas was in line with the change of attitude that we have noted above. He was henceforth not disposed to attack an institution which, as he himself has so clearly shown, was an effective barrier to too-rapid social change.

As Clemenceau conceived it the first task of the Republic was a purely negative one, systematically to destroy the influence of royalism in society. We have selected two examples, those of the Church and the Senate, to illustrate the campaign

---

51 *Ibid.*

52 Only the measures agreed upon in advance were actually passed by the Assembly. They included such trifling changes as the suppression of public prayers at the opening of the parliamentary session and the disbarment of members of the royal families from the office of President of the Republic.

which he waged during his early political career for the root-
ing out of ideas and institutions that belonged to the past and
for the establishment of a democratic Republic.

To whom did Clemenceau appeal to carry on the struggle
for his radical program? In whose interests did he conceive
that the Republic, once established, should exist? The answers
to these questions bring us to the heart of Clemenceau's concept of the Republic, of its social base, and of the relationship
of the classes within it.

IV

During the seventies and eighties Clemenceau, as we have
already seen, enjoyed considerable popularity among the working people. Indeed, there was not a little in the record to justify
the confidence thus placed in him. In 1876, when the organized
strength of the proletariat had been shattered by the defeat of
the *Commune* and by the reign of terror which followed it,
Clemenceau constituted himself the parliamentary spokesman
of labor. His maiden speech in the Chamber was a defense of
the *Communards* and a plea for amnesty which reinforced the
popular campaign then being undertaken, and had national re-
verberations. In 1879 he raised the demand for amnesty again
and championed the rights of Auguste Blanqui, the veteran
socialist agitator.[53] This parliamentary struggle, together with
Clemenceau's impassioned orations in defense of the Republic
and of egalitarian democracy reflected the political desires and
aspirations of the working people.

It would be a great mistake to conclude from these facts that
Clemenceau even then identified himself with the proletariat or
their interests. The contrary was the case. The industrial

53 Blanqui was imprisoned in 1871 for his part in the Paris insurrection
of October 30, 1870, and never amnestied. Eight years later he was elected
as deputy for Bordeaux but was promptly declared ineligible by the election
committee of the Chamber. Clemenceau led the radicals in demanding that
Blanqui be released from jail and be accorded his seat in the Assembly.
He carried on a parliamentary campaign around this issue for a number of
weeks (May to June 1879) with great persistence and oratorical skill.

workers in the towns and the great mass of poor peasants and day workers in the countryside neither owned property nor had any prospects of doing so. They were, in fact, instinctively antagonistic to the propertied classes and possessed latent revolutionary tendencies for which Clemenceau had learnt to fear and distrust them. In 1885 he confided in his *protégé* General Boulanger that ever since his experiences in Paris at the time of the *Commune* ". . . I, a Jacobin, have had a profound horror of riot and its extremes." [54] He detested the brilliant Jean Jaurès, that most moderate representative of the working class, as ". . . a fanatic, behind whose idyllic pictures you could always see rising the smoke of civil war." [55] In numerous passages-at-arms with socialist hecklers [56] at his political meetings he made it brutally clear that he would never subscribe to the Marxist ideals which, thanks to the tireless propaganda of Jules Guesde and his cohorts, were becoming dominant among the French working class during the eighties.

If Clemenceau for a while championed the interests of the proletariat, it was, as we shall see below, for reasons of his own. In the early years of the Republic his sympathies and affinities were above all with the small property owners. It was their interests which he considered the regime should reflect, and it was to them that he looked for political support. They played a pivotal part in his social philosophy. [57]

Clemenceau was brought up in a country district and had been accustomed since youth to go for long rambles through forest and over field. He had acquired the keenest knowledge of the life of the peasantry, and in his writings he glorified

---

54 Quoted by Daudet, *op. cit.*, 60.

55 *Clemenceau: the events of his life, op. cit.*, 280.

56 See above, 134 fn.

57 The characterization which Lafargue made of Victor Hugo is precisely applicable to Clemenceau. The *petite bourgeoisie* saw in him ". . . une des plus parfaites et des plus brillantes personnifications de ses instincts, de ses passions, et de ses pensées." *Critiques littéraires* (Paris, 1936), 124.

their harsh and narrow existence.[58] He found, or thought he found, in the peasant and his century-old routine a social force that was immune both to the idea and to the reality of change.

> The peasant [he wrote] lives in the miracle of the earth without seeing it, without understanding it. Rooted to his plot, he repeats the slow labor of his ancestors without any other goal than the winning of his daily bread, without any other prospect but that the days shall roll on until the earth, the object of all his toil, shall claim him too for its prey.[59]

Granted that society had undergone profound evolutions since the days of the cave-man,[60] Clemenceau nonetheless thought and hoped that the radical transformation of French agriculture still lay far off in the future. He considered that the small farmers were a stable group who would hold in check the revolutionary proletariat of the towns and mining districts.[61] " France, and above all rural France," he exclaimed, " which is the real France constituting the bulk of Frenchmen is, and will always remain, steadfastly individualistic, founded on *property, property, property.*" [62]

It might be pointed out that almost every item in this last contention was incorrect. In the first place, to say that rural France constituted " the bulk of Frenchmen " might be true, but it would conceal the underlying trends. From the middle of the nineteenth century until the end of the Third Republic the total French population increased from about thirty-five to

58 "...the ploughmen," he wrote, "hail each other on the way to work, urge on their beasts with cries, or hold them back with oaths, or brighten the day with songs of love. Soon they will be turning up the soil to that eternal obbligato of cries, oaths, songs, followed by a wheeling flock of birds in quest of food." *Les Plus Belles Pages* (Paris, 1908), 85.

59 *Figures de Vendée* (Paris, 1930), 56.

60 Clemenceau's philosophy of history was a crude mixture of social Darwinism and Nietzschean pessimism. It was set forth in the articles of *petite philosophie* which were collected in *La Mêlée sociale* (Paris, 1895).

61 H. M. Hyndman, *op. cit.*, 143.

62 *Ibid.*, 130. Italics not in original.

thirty-eight millions, but the *rural* population declined from about twenty-seven to twenty millions. Inexorably with the growth of industrialization people were drifting away from the rural areas. The disintegration of the old agrarian society was taking place.

In the second place rural France, even in Clemenceau's time, was founded upon the anonymous labor of a vast mass of landless or almost landless peasantry. It has long been a widespread belief that France under the Third Republic was the country *par excellence* of the small, prosperous, independent peasant farm. But in reality such was not the case. According to the census of 1906 two million, or nearly forty per cent of all French farmers, owned plots of land under two and one-half acres in size, plots so small that they did not suffice for the support of the owners and their families. Two and one-half million more owned tiny farms of from two to twenty-five acres. In 1912 Compère-Morel estimated that four million out of six and one-half million French farmers were landless, or semi-landless workers, compelled to hire themselves out whole or part-time to others in order to earn a living.[63] There was, it is true, a class of well-to-do farmers who owned or operated large or medium-sized properties: but in 1906 these constituted only a minority of the rural population, less than one million, or sixteen per cent of all cultivators. Clemenceau was idealizing as " the real France " a very limited and not at all representative group of farmers.

In the course of time the latter repaid the compliment and became the principle support of the Radical Party. But as a social type the well-to-do farmer did not stand alone in the France of those days. He shared the outlook and the inclinations of many other groups of *petit bourgeois* in the Third

63 *La Question agraire et le socialisme en France* (Paris, 1912), 54, 55. The impoverishment of the peasantry may be gauged from the fact that farmers with twenty-five acres of land or less constituted in 1929 nearly seventy-five per cent of all farmers, but they owned *less than twenty-five per cent* of all land.

Republic. Usually he was an employer, hiring wage-workers the year round and his poorer neighbors at harvest time. He was almost certain to be a *rentier* who had put his life savings into government bonds or the Russian loan. In this he closely resembled the petty ex-official, shopkeeper or clerical worker who after a lifetime of penurious scraping had retired to the countryside to live off his *rentes* and the vegetables which he grew in the back garden. In France the petty *rentier*, official, peasant, employer, and shopkeeper blended together. They held a position in the social scale intermediate between the landless or almost landless masses on the one side and the very wealthy classes on the other.

Clemenceau held out to this class, to the *petite bourgeoisie*, the prospect of a stable, democratic regime purged of the nefarious influence of the royalists and the Church. At the same time, in the late seventies, he was compelled to define clearly his attitude toward the proletariat. Neo-Jacobinism, in the first place, was at that time committed to a bitter fight with the opportunists on the issues both of foreign policy and of the organization of the state. Clemenceau understood that this fight could not be won without the aid of labor or, at the very least, that its success would be jeopardized if the workers followed an independent, revolutionary line.[64] In the second place, as we have already mentioned,[65] the late seventies witnessed the rapid revival of the socialist movement. Its most brilliant leaders were Jules Guesde, Paul Lafargue and the able group of propagandists and organizers which they gathered around them. By means of debates, speeches and articles the Guesdists carried on a vigorous polemic against Clemenceau. They struggled for years, and with a great deal of success, to educate the proletariat in Marxist, collectivist ideals. They carried on elec-

64 Clemenceau insisted that, if reaction were to be overthrown, all republicans would be "... compelled to march hand in hand and to present a common front against the enemy." *Discours de M. Clemenceau: Cirque Fernando*, October 30, 1882.

65 See above, 123, 133-134.

toral campaigns which were waged around the demand for immediate social reforms. This agitation exerted a powerful influence upon the workers, particularly in the industrial regions of the North and Center. As early as 1880 the Guesdists were challenging in the sharpest fashion Clemenceau's leadership of the working class. Definition of the relationship of the latter to the neo-Jacobin *petite bourgeoisie* became essential if the Guesdists' challenge was to be met.

The position which Clemenceau assumed on this issue in the early eighties contained two elements. The first was an insistence that radicals and socialists had a common interest in political unity for the sake of the struggle against the royalists, clericals and opportunists. Defense of the Republic was the link that must bind together all republicans, and social aims must be subordinated to this.[66] More concretely put, this was an appeal for working-class support in the radical campaign against the bureaucracy, against clerical influence in the schools and against the constitution of 1875.

From the contention that the radical Republic was in the interest of the proletariat as much as of the neo-Jacobins, and that it was, in fact, a condition for social advance, Clemenceau appealed for a unity of both classes under radical leadership. The Guesdists were in agreement with Clemenceau on the point that the Republic provided the most favorable terrain for organizing the workers.[67] But they sharply opposed the contention that therefore the socialists should unite with the radicals and follow their lead. On the contrary Guesde insisted that the interests of the two groups diverged fundamentally; the aim of the socialists was to organize the workers into " an independent force capable of shattering the existing social order." [68]

66 " What you should work for," he said, " is the regime of political liberty which alone can pave the way for social advance." *Cirque Fernando, op. cit.*, April 11, 1880.

67 *Égalité*, July 21, 1880.

68 *Ibid.*

Therefore the second element in Clemenceau's position was of necessity the contention that radicalism provided a path of peaceful social reform which would satisfy the aspirations of the proletariat and render revolution unnecessary.

Clemenceau started from the assumption that it was futile and dangerous to rely upon force alone to cow the workers and check their struggles. He referred to Thiers, who bore the main historical responsibility for crushing the *Commune* as ". . . the savage, limited type of *bourgeois* who steeps himself in blood without flinching." [69] The civil war of 1871 appeared to him as a criminal mistake because it stored up undying resentment in the people and made the task of 'social conciliation' a difficult one. The main theme of his speech on the *Commune* in 1876 was the contention that the clash of 1871 was not the fault of the Parisians and could have been avoided if Thiers had not been stupidly determined to stamp out the capital's resistance by force. " I tell you," he said, " that instead of admitting that you are compelled at certain times to indulge in pitiless repression, you must make the resolution to win these men [the workers] to the cause of peaceful reform. . . ." [70]

Until 1880 Clemenceau considered that 'reform' was essentially a political concept. He gave little attention to social reform. But in May of that year the Guesdists prepared their program for the coming elections in 1881, and it was ratified at a regional conference of the Socialist Party held in Paris in July. The principal demands which the Guesdists made were for a reduction of the legal maximum hours of work, a ban on child labor in the factories and mines, old-age pensions, abolition of the *livret,* accident insurance, and recognition of the right to organize.[71]

69 *Clemenceau: the events of his life, op. cit.,* 279.

70 *Journal officiel (Chambre des Deputés),* 1876, 3341.

71 *Égalité,* June 30, 1880. This *Programme electoral des Travailleurs socialistes* was the joint work of Marx, Engels, Guesde, and Lafargue. The *livret* was a workbook which workers had been legally obliged to carry with them since the time of Napoleon I. It facilitated police control of labor organizers and the blacklisting of the latter by employers.

Clemenceau's reply to this challenge was swift. He formed a *radical-socialist* wing of his party entitled the *Alliance socialiste républicaine* headed by Charles Longuet and some of the most moderate *ex-Communards*.[72] In its opening manifesto the *Alliance* appealed to socialists of whatever school " to unite upon a basis of political action and of practical reforms that are immediately realizable." The electoral program of the *Alliance* was published in October 1880. It bore a close resemblance to Guesde's. Four days later Clemenceau commented upon these ' minimum demands ' in a speech made before a working-class audience at Marseille.[73] He again called for unity of all republicans on the issue of consolidating the Republic, but added that radicals and socialists could also agree upon certain immediate social reforms. On this basis he invited the workers to abandon any ulterior objectives, such as revolution and collectivism, and to join forces with the radicals.

The position taken by Clemenceau that socialist parties should not question the existing order, but should press only for gradual improvements in the people's condition of life, has become known as " social reformism." In subsequent years he elaborated it considerably. In 1882, he told his electors that " if one wants the political and economic order to be changed by peaceful means, it is necessary to give the underprivileged the impression that the betterment of their lot is the constant concern of their representatives." [74] In 1884, speaking before the Chamber of Deputies on the economic crisis, he said that under certain conditions he was in favor of state intervention in economic life. " I ask you," he said, " to intervene with subsidies wherever necessary to protect the worker against un-

---

72 Longuet was a collaborator of Clemenceau on *La Justice,* and son-in-law of Marx. The *Alliance* was a shortlived organization and dissolved in 1881, some of its members remaining with the radicals, others going over to Guesde. For further details see Alexandre Zévaès, *Histoire du socialisme et du communisme en France* (Paris, 1947), 113 ff.; and Georges Weill, *Histoire du mouvement sociale en France* (Paris, 1924), 236.

73 *Discours de M. Clemenceau: Théâtre des Nations, op. cit.*

74 *Cirque Fernando, op. cit.,* October 30, 1882.

employment, illness, old age, against all the accidents to which he is liable. I ask that you take measures to defend men against the economic and social institutions which oppress them. . . ." [75]

The reforms to which Clemenceau referred would cost money; his suggestions were received with a noticeable lack of enthusiasm. But Clemenceau insisted, in terms that even for him were unusually blunt, that the alternatives were clear between reform and revolution.[76] It was a question of establishing ". . . under what legal and equitable conditions the state can intervene, without harming individual initiative, in order to secure a more just distribution of wealth. . . ." [77] Sooner or later, he concluded, the question must be posed in these terms or "it will end in violence."

Clemenceau foretold correctly. Social reformism had become by the end of the century a fundamental policy of the radicals. The latter felt the need to revise their traditional *laissez-faire* principles in the light of their new practice. They found a *rationale* for it in the social philosophy of *solidarité* which became popular with the middle class after 1900. In the next chapter some account of the origins and significance of this philosophy will be given.

75 *Débats parlementaires (Chambre des Deputés)*, 1884, I, 257.

76 " Let the issue be faced squarely [at the elections] ! We will not say : 'We must make a revolution, cut the throats of the *bourgeoisie*, expropriate the owners.' We will say : 'A glaring social and economic injustice exists : some are too poor and some are too rich.' That's what we will say." At this point the outraged Jules Ferry broke in to exclaim " Never before has anyone used such language from the podium ! " *Ibid.*, 258.

77 *Loc. cit.*

CHAPTER II

SOLIDARITÉ—AN OFFICIAL PHILOSOPHY

TOWARD the end of the nineteenth century neo-Jacobinism began to come into its own. Two years after Clemenceau's electoral defeat of 1893 a cabinet formed exclusively of radicals took office. In 1901 the Radical and Radical-Socialist Party was constituted as a permanent political organization. In the elections of the following year it secured over two hundred seats in the Chamber of Deputies and became the dominant parliamentary group.

As they advanced toward political power the radicals began to lay more stress upon their social program. As we have seen, pressure from the Left had already affected the radical electoral program in 1881 and in subsequent years. This had little immediate effect owing to the rise of the Boulangist movement in the late eighties. Boulangism seriously interfered with the normal evolution of the political parties, but by the early nineties the labor movement in particular was beginning to recover from this transient crisis. Socialist deputies, in the persons of Jules Guesde, Jean Jaurès and others began to apply pressure for the passage of social legislation. The radicals themselves were not unmindful of the fact that France lagged far behind other West European countries, notably Germany and Switzerland, in this respect. They followed the policy, previously enunciated by Clemenceau, of allying with the Left against the Center and the Right, and there developed accordingly a movement for the passage of certain fundamental laws to alleviate the worst evils of industrial life. The beginning of this period was marked in 1892 by the passage of a law that regulated the conditions of employment of women and children in the factories.[1] During the next decade French labor legisla-

1 This law extended and revived a largely ineffective law of 1874.

tion made no very conspicuous advances but it grew steadily in volume.[2]

This system of legislation established machinery for the enforcement of its provisions, encouraged the growth of administrative law, and provided for financial contributions from employer and taxpayer for the payment of new officials and the operation of the new insurance schemes. One result of this was that the radicals found themselves placed in a false position. They had inherited traditional republican ideas on the sanctity of property, the rights of individual enterprise, and the blessings of *laissez-faire*, but had done little under Clemenceau's leadership to modify their principles and to bring them into consonance with the changed political situation. Accused by their adversaries of having entered upon the slippery path of state socialism, they found that the measures which they were being compelled to support were in practical conflict with their ideas. Social legislation empirically undertaken thus raised sharply the question as to the *limits* of this type of action and as to the principles which should guide its formulation.[3] Evidently, a new statement was required which would express the wedding of radicalism with social reform that had originally taken place under the aegis of Clemenceau; and which would rally radicals and socialists to the support of reform policies.

2 Principal landmarks in this legislative history were: the law of 1893 regulating safety conditions in workshops; the law of 1894 on compulsory insurance for miners; the law of 1898 establishing the principle of employers' liability for industrial accidents; and the law of 1905 on old age pensions and insurance. See Raoul Jay, *La Protection légale des travailleurs* (Paris, 1910), and Paul Pic, *Les Assurances sociales en France et à l'étranger* (Paris, 1913).

3 The embarrassment caused the radical-socialists by the lack of a consistent doctrine on labor policy is evident in Paul Pic's early work, *Traité élémentaire de législation industrielle* (Paris, 1894). Radicals are here identified as members of an empirical or eclectic school; they are described as those who "limit themselves to establishing, on the basis of experience, that the state can to some extent regularize industrial progress," and thus, by means of intervention, forestall "those conflicts that would be produced both by systematic non-intervention and by excess of regulation." (Page 16).

By the end of the nineteenth century this formulation had been achieved in the philosophy of *solidarité*. This doctrine, which attempted to reconcile the conflicting ideas of *laissez-faire* and state intervention in economic life, might correctly be characterized as a mere piece of shallow eclecticism.[4] It might be argued that it was of little account in intellectual history. But this judgment would fail to give a true picture of *solidarité* as the expression of neo-Jacobin predominance in French political and intellectual life. After the turn of the century this doctrine was widely propagated in the Assembly and the press, in the schools and the universities. It not only became a quasi-official republican philosophy but it deeply affected thought and teaching on many social subjects. Its influence, in fact, might easily be traced upon jurisprudence, social legislation, economic theory, sociology and many more. But to do this would require a study in itself. The following essay is confined to outlining the origins and mature expression of *solidarité* as a republican doctrine, and to sketching the principal factors that governed its development.

I

Alfred Fouillée (1838-1912) was the founder of French solidarist philosophy. He began his work in the early seventies and by the end of the century had brought together all the elements that were with certain corrections to be compounded into the system of *solidarité*. Fouillée [5] was a professional philosopher of Breton origin. When he was nineteen years old his plans for a university education were interrupted by the death of his father. He became the sole support of his family and

---

4 Arthur W. Spencer noted that Fouillée, who, as we shall see, was one of the pioneers of *solidarité*, achieved "...not a real synthesis, but only a mélange of seemingly opposed philosophical tendencies." *Modern French Legal Philosophy* (Modern Legal Philosophy Series, vol. VII, Boston, 1916), xxxix.

5 The following biographical details have been borrowed from Élisabeth Ganne de Beaucoudrey, *La Psychologie et la métaphysique des idées-forces chez Alfred Fouillée* (Paris, 1936); Augustin Guyau, *La Philosophie et la sociologie d'Alfred Fouillée* (Paris, 1913); and François Maury, *Figures et aspects de Paris* (Paris, 1910).

spent a painful youth as a high school pedagogue and university lecturer struggling, amidst other responsibilities, to take higher educational degrees and to win professional recognition. Before the fall of the Second Empire Fouillée came to the attention of the philosophical world as a result of his work on Plato.[6] But his real *début* was made before a wider public in 1872, when he created a sensation in the defense of his doctoral dissertation at the Sorbonne. It is related that Gambetta, who was present on this occasion, was so impressed by Fouillée's charm and eloquence that he offered him a political career and a seat in the Chamber of Deputies, both of which Fouillée refused.[7]

These promising beginnings were cut short in 1875 by a physical breakdown which forced Fouillée into premature retirement. He settled on the Riviera and devoted the rest of his long life to the writing of numerous books and articles developing his views on philosophy, history, psychology and many other subjects. He became known for his theory of *ideas as determinative forces,* a theory of causation that exercized no small influence upon Bergson, Nietzsche and Weber, to name only the most prominent. His work was characterized by an undisciplined abundance, a tiresome repetition, a diffuseness of ideas and a lack of systematic exposition. But his influence upon the radical republicans was enormous. He was the first man to bring together and to discuss exhaustively the principal elements out of which later developed the mature doctrine of *solidarité.*

Fouillée's thought [8]—and indeed the thought of all radical

6 In two competitions promoted by the Academy of Moral and Political Sciences on the theory of Platonic ideas and the philosophy of Socrates Fouillée received first prize *cum laude.*

7 Renouvier said of him, according to Guyau, that "in comparison with such a fund of eloquence the boasted lessons of Victor Cousin were contemptible."

8 Élisabeth Ganne de Beaucoudrey, *op. cit.,* contains a complete bibliography of Fouillée's works and a chronological listing of his articles. This work, and Guyau, *op. cit.,* provide an extended commentary on the political and philosophical aspects of Fouillée's thought.

republicans after 1880—was deeply influenced by the theories of social Darwinism. The 1870's had witnessed the introduction into France of ideas that first challenged and then swept away many of the older political conceptions. The principal protagonist of these ideas was Herbert Spencer, who applied the notion of the survival of the fittest to society as a justification of *laissez-faire;* and popularized the idea of society as a living organism with division of function and centralized control. A number of works, based upon these and similar teachings, enjoyed a wide vogue in France at this time, notably Éspinas' *Des Sociétés animales,*[9] and Albert Schäffle's *Bau und Leben des sozialen Körpers.*[10]

These teachings were seized upon to buttress traditionalist concepts of society and state; their value for royalist and conservative apologetics was obvious.[11] But such ideas contradicted the fundamental position of the republicans, and above all of the radicals. If society was merely an animal organism, and the state merely its 'brain,' or central control, no place was left for the theory of democracy; rather a society of robots and a dictatorial state was indicated. If, too, the laws of natural selection and survival of the fittest, applied to society, indicated a policy of *laissez-faire,* there was no place, obviously, for state intervention in economic life, for the development of a state social policy. Refutation of this viewpoint, or some form of reconciliation with it, became imperative for radical-socialism.

9 Paris, 1877.

10 Tübingen, 1875.

11 Students of French conservatism during this period have concentrated upon the more repulsive manifestations—chauvinism, antisemitism, and so forth—of reactionary thought. They have largely neglected to investigate the inroads of Spencerian dogma upon the social science and philosophy of the period. The impact of social Darwinism upon German authoritarian thought has received rather more attention. Schäffle's importance in this respect has been stressed by Ralph Bowen, *German Theories of the Corporative State* (New York, 1947), chapter 4.

Fouillée's answer to the challenge of the social Darwinists appeared in 1880 under the title *La Science sociale contemporaine*. The problem was here presented in the form of an antithesis between the social contract theory of Rousseau and the historical and naturalistic schools represented by Comte and Spencer. Whereas, Fouillée pointed out, Rousseau's theory assumed free will on the part of a number of individuals to come together and to associate in a democratic society, Comte and Spencer taught that human communities were historically or biologically determined, or rather, that they were conditioned by factors extraneous to the human will. " Social contract and social organism," he wrote, " these then are the two ideas which today confront one another and whose reconciliation seems at first sight to be impossible." [12]

Was society something that had grown up by a spontaneous evolution, something therefore, which it was beyond human power to constitute or to change? Or was there a place in it for human self-determination and freedom of association? Such was the question that Fouillée considered radical philosophy was called upon to answer.

His solution to this problem lay in an attempt to reconcile and to combine the traditional contractual theory with the new data of biology.[13] Examining the criticism that had been levelled at the contract theory, he insisted that it must be interpreted, not as a historical account of how society had been formed, but as a purely rational justification of existing association. Free contract or the unforced agreement of individuals was for Fouillée the only reasonable basis of social life. Men, he considered, consciously adhered to this contract when, by reaching the age of reason, they agreed to go on living in the state and to accept its laws. " From the legal point of view," he concluded, " it is necessary that society be considered as a vast associative contract, the most general of all, within which

12 *La Science sociale contemporaine* (3rd edition, 1885), xi.

13 "...the theories of free contract and organic evolution," he wrote, " seem to us to be inseparable." *Ibid.*, xii.

other agreements will find their place and their guarantees." [14]
Fouillée, in other words, was saying that, while the social contract could not be interpreted as a serious explanation of *how*
society has come into being, men nevertheless continued to act
as if they were bound to each other by a preexisting agreement.
He added that this was above all true in democratic societies,
whose constitutional arrangements, notably universal suffrage,
he described as nothing more than " the solemn renewal of the
social contract."

Fouillée was here defining social contract in a special sense as
a rational justification of society to which all individuals in it
gave implicit sanction by their continued presence in that particular community. He continued to use the term social contract
for this particular interpretation. In later works, however, he
began to use the legal term *quasi-contract* to convey the same
meaning.[15] Though he never generalized the use of this term,
he originated its application to social theory. Quasi-contract,
both as a concept and a phrase, was to play a significant part
in later solidarist theory as developed by Léon Bourgeois.

Having done justice to the idealist school of political philosophy—and, indeed, in the above the influence of Plato is as
obvious as that of Rousseau—Fouillée went on to appraise the
work of the social Darwinists: " now," he wrote, " that the
natural sciences are justly held in honor, it is in their domain
that authoritarian systems are continually seeking new and
more refined arguments. It is there also that liberals must look
for support for their theories." [16] Quickly rejecting the notion,
held notably by Éspinas, that society possessed a national
spirit, or conscience, over and above that of the individuals
composing it, Fouillée attempted to show, nonetheless, that
society was analogous to an organism, and was, in fact, " a real

14 *Ibid.*, 13.

15 See, for instance, Fouillée's treatment of the state's obligations to
orphans and the aged in *La Propriété sociale* (Paris, 1885), 132.

16 *Science sociale, op. cit.*, 77.

living being." In both societies and organisms there was specialization of functions, and, conversely, their solidarity and cooperation for a final end. Organization, he said, involved division of labor and hence specialization. The resulting unity or *social solidarity* had as its result cooperation, or " common effort for a final end which is the maintenance of the whole." [17] Society, further, according to him, was not merely organized like a living creature, it was actually alive, since it was composed of living units, or individuals, in the same way as an organism was composed of smaller living parts. Postulating a struggle for life and the mutual interaction of individuals in this struggle, Fouillée combined—artificially enough, no doubt —the idea of the mutual dependence of living beings in society with a continual struggle of each of them for survival.[18]

So far Fouillée followed Spencer. However, he combined this conception of society as an organism with the theory of the social contract to reach conclusions very different from those of the Englishman. At what moment, he asked, does a gathering of individuals become a society? His answer was, at that moment when " all these men conceive more or less clearly a type of organism which they could form in uniting, and when they unite effectively under the influence of this conception." [19] This union of men, of their own free will, in an association characterized by mutual dependence of all individuals in the community, that is, characterized by a high degree of social solidarity, Fouillée termed a *contractual organism.* In a modified form this curious idea—or blending of opposite ideas—was to constitute the basis of the solidarist conception of society.

Fouillée went on to ask how conflict, produced in society by the struggle for life, might be resolved. The principal cause of such conflicts was, of course, the exercize of property rights, which concentrated wealth in a small number of hands, making " a monopoly out of the instruments of production and thus

17 *Ibid.*, 80.
18 *Ibid.*, 91.
19 *Ibid.*, 115.

depriving men of their right to work." From these conflicts arose the central problem of social theory; how to prevent the collisions arising from the maldistribution of property, and how to repair them once they had occurred.

On this latter question, Fouillée, and indeed, neo-Jacobin thought in general, had nothing new to add to Renouvier's formulations on the "state of war" and society's right to defend itself against predatory acts.[20] It was the former aspect of the problem—that is, how to avoid collisions between labor and capital—that led to the statement of the most characteristic elements in Fouillée's solidarist theory. Renouvier and Secrétan had pointed out that ownership of property led to injustice and the violation of human rights. According to traditional Christian philosophy the resulting injustices were repaired by the obligations of charity and benevolence. But Fouillée was looking for a juridical basis for state intervention in economic life: for this purpose the traditional Christian teaching, based upon purely personal moral precepts, was bound to be inadequate. The Christian idea of fraternity and charity, he said, was no longer applicable to the conditions of society, because it was mystical in nature, "a mere sentiment, subject to errors and abusive interpretations, and without scientific or juridical exactness." It failed to provide criteria for *state* intervention to remedy industrial wrongs, because it enjoined only *personal* benevolence and welldoing. Fouillée thus rejected specifically the mystical feeling of human solidarity and brotherhood upon which Renouvier and after him Marion had based the cohesion of society. Private benevolence was well enough in primitive societies; its place, in Fouillée's scheme, was taken by the idea of ' justice,' which, growing even more forceful as men struggled to realize it, dictated the replacement of charity by *public* philanthropic action.

20 Fouillée described Renouvier's treatment of the state of war as "the dominating and most original idea of his work." *Science sociale, op. cit.,* 362 fn.

According to this way of thinking justice itself was the product of evolution, of men's struggles to realize an ideal ever present in their minds.[21] As the idea of right, of justice, made progress, pure charity, according to Fouillée, was left an ever smaller field within which to operate. Justice now began to assume the obligation of *reparation,* that is, of making up to those who had been wronged for the deprivations which they had suffered. Conflicts arose because owing to the concentration of landed property and capital a propertyless class had come into existence that could not provide for its own security. This wrong, thought Fouillée, might be redressed by the intervention of justice, or of what he termed 'public benevolence.' According to this conception justice must be considered as an active, positive force that " was obliged to do good in order to repair the evil that has been done."[22] The need for such 'reparative justice' he considered a permanent one in modern society. " There is, " he concluded, " a certain amount of general injustice which is imputable, not to any particular individual, but to society in its entirety, and this is often the legacy of the past. Hence the necessity for reparative justice."[23] It would, he thought, remain a requisite so long as the Rousseauan concept of the state as an ideal association among free and equal men was " denatured by a struggle for life which provokes people to egoism and wrong-doing." [24]

Here emerges, in Fouillée's thought, yet another of the main features of solidarist philosophy; one, further, which enables us to establish the relationship of ' justice ' and ' solidarity ' in this system with a good deal of precision. *Solidarity and justice are quite distinct. Solidarité* with him is not, as with Marion

21 This combination of idealism and evolution Fouillée achieved by means of his concept of the *idée-force.* The theory of the *idée-force* was an important part of his system but treatment of it is beyond the purpose of the present essay.

22 *Science sociale, op. cit.,* 356.

23 *Loc. cit.*

24 *Ibid.,* 358.

and Renouvier, a sentiment, a feeling of brotherly love for one's fellows, but a 'scientific fact,' resulting from the organisation of society as a living evolving creature with division of labor and central organisation of functions. Justice, on the other hand, is an ideal concept, supposed to embody a social obligation to make amends to members of society who have suffered wrong through violation of their right to property. The *juridical* basis for the fulfilment of such obligation lies, as has been seen, in the supposed contract that binds individuals together in society and gives them a legal title to certain rights and benefits. In general, the obligation flows from the idea of a 'social debt' arising between the principal groups in the community and resulting from economic operations and the maladjustments of social life. This debt must be discharged, under the terms of the contract, if conflict is not to arise. Hence the term 'reparative justice,' justice that repairs, by acts of positive legislation, injuries inflicted upon members of society in the past or as the result of existing economic conditions.

Fouillée went on to deal with the question of the agency that would determine and carry out reparative justice. Charity had been the function of individuals, but obviously its modern counterpart could not be handled in the same way. Since, he said, " in the political and social sphere men are *collectively* unjust, the state must repair the evils that society has committed." Society, he considered, could no longer be thought of as an entity absolved of all responsibility for the social consequences of the economic process, but must step in " to fix the amount of the indemnification for damage suffered by the individual." Reparation of this sort, he concluded, was an obligation of the members of society taken collectively, i.e. was a *state* obligation.

Such, in essentials, was the neo-Jacobin doctrine first elaborated by Fouillée. Its practical implications were developed, in timid and tentative fashion, in Fouillée's next work on social theory, *Social Property and Democracy*.[25] Here he launched a

25 *La Propriété sociale et la démocratie* (Paris, 1884).

frontal attack on social Darwinism as an apologia for *laissez-faire*, and developed the reasons why the idea of a struggle for survival might be used, on the contrary, to justify state intervention in social life. The Darwinists had justified non-interference on the grounds that natural selection would eliminate the 'unfit.' Fouillée pointed out that this latter term could apply only to a very small number of people in a modern community; he stressed that 'unfitness' was not a natural condition due to the maladaptation of the organism to its surroundings but was, for the most part, artificially induced by defects in the environment itself. State intervention that would mitigate and remedy poor living and working conditions could not possibly be harmful, since it would improve standards of 'fitness,' and give men a better chance to survive; it would not, as the Darwinists implied, merely perpetuate a race of weaklings.[26]

Granted then that state intervention, 'public philanthropy,' must be pursued, to whom should it be addressed and to what extent? Fouillée's ideas here foreshadowed in a tentative way the future legislative program of the Radical Party. The state, he considered, owed assistance first of all to orphans, and to others like the invalid or the aged who were incapable of supporting themselves. He also recognized the necessity of instituting insurance for the workers against the principal hazards of life—accident and illness, old age and unemployment.

Fouillée's doctrine of state intervention as an instrument of social reform was developed to combat the collectivist idea that all productive wealth, originally the property of the community, had been stolen from it by landlords and capitalists, and must be restored to it before the roots of social inequality could be

26 " What would one say," he asked, " of a father who in order to develop the strength of his children, had then accustom themselves to go without food; who, in order to develop their lungs, placed them in an unventilated room, and who, in order to develop their keenness of sight, made them work and read without proper illumination? " But, he argued, it was exactly this position that the social Darwinists were taking in opposing state intervention to improve industrial conditions. *Ibid.*, 97.

destroyed. He boasted that his theory combined the best features of liberalism and socialism while avoiding the pitfalls of both. Be that as it may, in *solidarité* as he originated it may be seen a social outlook that attempted to straddle these two opposed positions and to achieve some sort of reconciliation between them. Fouillée advocated the maintenance of private enterprise and the rights of private property; but he thought that concessions should be made to alleviate the worst, the most crying evils of industrialism. His position squarely reflected the interests of the *petite bourgeoisie* midway between big business and labor; this group was concerned both to maintain the capitalist system and to head off the revolutionary movement by a policy of partial reforms. Fouillée's work gave a philosophical formulation to the position for which Clemenceau had campaigned from 1876 to 1893 and which, in general, expressed the political and social objectives of radical-socialism. He thus performed no small service in developing a neo-Jacobin ideology and in clarifying its relationship to other parties and philosophical systems.

Toward the end of the century, as radicalism increased in popular influence and parliamentary strength, the need was felt to bring the diverse elements of the radical creed into a consistent statement of the party position; one, that is, that was not hidden away in abstruse philosophical tomes, but that would be readily available for political use, and that would be easily comprehensible to the general public. This task was performed by Léon Bourgeois, a leading radical politician and parliamentary spokesman. To this work and its significance in radical thought some attention must now be given.

II

Léon Bourgeois [27] (1851-1925) followed in his early years

27 Biographical material will be found in *Polybiblion*, CII (1925), 303; M. Hamburger, *Hommes politiques* (Paris, 1932); and, above all, in *Hommage à l'apôtre de la solidarité et de la paix: inauguration du monument élevé à la mémoire de Léon Bourgeois par M. Albert Lebrun, Président de la République* (Châlons-sur-Marne, 1933).

a career that was typical enough of many a pushing young radical politician in the first generation of the Third Republic. Bourgeois fought in the Franco-German war and subsequently studied law. Thus equipped he entered the administrative service in 1876 as a loyal follower of Gambetta. An intensely ambitious young man, he rose rapidly until his appointment in 1887 as Prefect of Police. Bourgeois' political career began in earnest the next year, when he defeated General Boulanger in a straight fight in the general election of 1888, and was elected Deputy for the Marne. Once in parliament Bourgeois was an immediate success : he was the type of politician who is, in the French term, eminently *ministrable,* that is, utilisable for almost any position in almost any cabinet. From 1888, when he became Secretary of State under Floquet, until the day of his death over a third of a century later, Bourgeois held one long succession of political posts as Minister for Home Affairs, Prime-Minister, Minister of Education, Minister for Foreign Affairs, and Minister of Labor. He was elected to the responsible position of President of the Chamber in 1902. When he graduated to the Senate three years later he was, along with Clemenceau, an acknowledged elder statesman of the recently constituted Radical and Radical-Socialist Party.[28]

The man, therefore, who first put forward his ideas on *solidarité* in 1896 [29] was no political tyro; he had headed the

28 Bourgeois also resembled Clemenceau in being a leading spokesman for the radicals on foreign affairs. A delegate to the Hague Peace Conference in 1898, he became in 1920 the first French representative to the League of Nations.

29 Bourgeois' book *Solidarité* (Paris, 1897), was originally given to the world in 1896 as a series of articles published in *La Nouvelle Revue;* and its main lines were also set forth in a speech of December 23, 1895, entitled "La politique de ceux qui pensent aux autres." The ideas set forth in *Solidarité* were further developed in two speeches, "La solidarité et la liberté," and "La solidarité et la justice," made in 1900 at the *Congrès internationale de l'éducation sociale;* and in two addresses, "L'idée de solidarité et ses conséquences sociales," and "Les applications de la solidarité sociale," given at the *École des hautes études sociales* in 1901 and 1902 respectively. These speeches with other relevant material are published in the seventh edition of *Solidarité* (Paris, 1912), to which reference will hereafter be made.

first all-radical cabinet in the history of the Third Republic and was a leading parliamentary figure. The repercussions of his work were immediate; the more so because to many people, ignorant of the long preparation which solidarist ideas had undergone in France, this new philosophy seemed to spring fully armed from the ground. Bourgeois' little book, *Solidarité*, was published in 1897 and immediately became popular. Taught in the colleges and schools, expounded and elaborated by a host of theorists, it remained the dominant philosophy of French republicanism until well after the close of the first World War. It inspired a flood of bills on social welfare, entire passages of which were often couched in Bourgeois' own phraseology. In this sense its impact on legislation was analogous to that of Benthamite utilitarianism earlier in the nineteenth century upon English penal reform.[30]

For Bourgeois the central problem of political theory was the formulation of those considerations that justified the application of legal sanctions to compel men to perform their social duties. The discoveries of Darwinism, he said, appeared to have given a powerful impetus to the liberal, individualist thesis; the struggle for existence seemed to explain and to justify the realities of ruthless social competition. But philosophers had not been long in opposing to this theory the doctrine of the solidarity of living beings, a doctrine which, in its turn, was borrowed from natural science, from the idea of the interdependence of elements in a living organism; and they had shown that an organic solidarity, based upon the

30 " It has been suggested," wrote Charles Gide in 1909, " that the social legislation of the last twenty years, such as the regulations governing the conditions of labor, factory and general hygiene, insurance against accidents and old age, State aid for the aged and disabled, ... all of which are the outcome of preaching solidarity ... should be known as 'the laws of social solidarity.'" Charles Gide and Charles Rist, *A History of Economic Doctrines* (Boston, n. d.), 601, 602. Note also Gaston Maurice's remark, " Le grand mérite du solidarisme fut de ramener fortement aux questions sociales le parti radical qui risquait de se faire éclipser par le socialisme." *Le Parti radical* (Paris, 1929), 27.

division of labor between the members of society, was at the basis of organized community life.[31]

Organic solidarity, the mutual interdependence of the members of society, was then a social fact. But taken by itself it could enlighten us little as to our duties to others or as to the legislative policies which ought to be followed. It still remained, thought Bourgeois, to formulate this solidarity as a juridical conception, to provide legal sanctions for the mutual obligations which might be deduced from this social principle. It remained to establish, " on the basis of the scientific doctrine of natural solidarity, a precise rule of the rights and duties of each in the communal life." [32]

Bourgeois' answer to this problem was an effort to reconcile the ideas of Christian liberalism on the one hand with the claims of socialism on the other. The liberals, in defending the individual from interference with his freedom of enterprise and his property, had insisted that aid to others, or charity, was not a matter for the state, but was a purely moral obligation, a personal matter between the giver and God. The socialists, on the contrary, had claimed that the sacred rights of property must be overridden in the interests of all, and that the state must step in to play a central part in the process of production and distribution of goods. Bourgeois agreed with the liberals that the traditional freedom of the individual was " the first condition of progress in society," but he added that the activities of the individual must necessarily be limited by the fact of association. Society—and here he was in cautious agreement with the socialists—" cannot remain indifferent to

31 The concept of organic solidarity based upon the division of labor was used by Fouillée, as has been seen; but it received much further elaboration and development in Émile Durkheim's dissertation De la division du travail social, which appeared in 1893. Durkheim's sociological theory influenced radical-socialist thought considerably, but it did not alter the main line of its development, the sketching of which is the main purpose of the present essay; it is, therefore, not considered in this place. For the relationship of Durkheim's work to the general philosophy of solidarité, see below, 183-184.

32 Solidarité, op. cit., 31, 32.

the blind play of economic phenomena, but must subordinate psychic, historical, and economic forces to its own requirements and must relate them to its own moral ends." [33] It must step in and force men to perform the social obligations which their sense of justice tells them instinctively that they should acknowledge.

Solidarité, then, as a theoretical study, was an investigation of the nature of human association as the basis of obligations which might justify legal intervention on behalf of the poor or oppressed members of society.[34] If it could be shown that society was the result of an agreement on the part of its members to promote justice for all, there would be little difficulty in arguing that state intervention was justified as a means of establishing and maintaining those conditions without which the contract of association must be considered void. Plainly, contract theory of the traditional type, which had been used to justify the *political* supremacy of the republican State during the Great Revolution, could be used equally effectively to justify it as a *social* agency under the Third Republic. But contract theory had been subjected to effective criticism since its heyday during the Convention; it foundered, Bourgeois pointed out, upon the objection that there was not, and could not be, an actual contract among the members of society. That the concept was historically unsound was hardly open to question.

Bourgeois did not, for all that, abandon the attempt to found society upon contract. He asserted that social life must be explained and laws formulated *as though* a contract did actually exist. In assuming this position Bourgeois was merely driving to a logical conclusion an idea which Fouillée had adumbrated before him but had not consistently applied. Society, Bourgeois argued, maintained itself not by an *open,* but by a *tacit* agreement among its members; and this, following Fouillée, he

33 *Ibid.,* 13, 14.
34 *Ibid.,* 6.

termed the *quasi-contract*. The concept was borrowed from the civil code where it was used traditionally to designate a contract agreed upon and recognized after the relationship in question had been established between the parties concerned. It was, thought Bourgeois, the nature of society to place men in relationships where they had been unable to discuss previously or in any way to arrange the terms of their association. But laws might be made to give effect to the agreement that men might have established among themselves if they had all been able to consult together freely beforehand. When agreement had been reached by such means, a quasi-contract had come into effect. " The quasi-contract," Bourgeois concluded, " is nothing else but the social contract retroactively adhered to." [35]

Bourgeois thus drove the social contract out by the front door only to admit it again by the back. The division of labor in society, he argued, and the solidarity—or interdependence —of men arising from this fact, created a contract of association which men were held to agree to by the mere act of continuing to live and work in the given community; the object of this contract, he considered, was that of any agreement freely entered into; namely, to establish that equivalence of services given and received which alone could guarantee the continued existence of the association.

In an ideal situation, continued Bourgeois, it would not be necessary to define the obligations arising out of the social contract, or to provide legal sanctions for them. This task was necessary precisely because the social situation was abnormal rather than ideal; the concentration of property had brought about class division and conflicts which it was necessary that society itself should resolve by its own action. The central problem of theory was thus to establish the nature and the extent of the legislative intervention which ought to be imposed upon men—or which they sought to consent to—in order to achieve this end.[36]

35 *Ibid.*, 61.

36 *Ibid.*, 32.

Under existing conditions, then, the exchange of services was not based upon equivalence; some members of society received more than their just due from the social arrangement: the balance must be paid if the contract was not to be repudiated. This concept of an equivalence of services as the basis of the social contract Bourgeois rendered concrete by an elaboration of Fouillée's idea of the social debt. Every individual, he said, discharged his obligations to society by rendering services in exchange for the benefits which he received: everyone, that is, owed toward all others living in the same society a debt for the services which they performed for him. "At the basis of all juridical obligation," he wrote, "public or private, lies the notion of a debt." [37] To Bourgeois it was axiomatic that the rich had not discharged their social debt and that, therefore, existing social arrangements were 'deformed,' and could not, without legal intervention, become the basis for a true or permanent social contract. Injustice did not merely arise from the natural inequality of human talents, a thing which it was beyond the scope of human legislation to remedy; it arose out of the historical situation under which society had come into being, from the usurpation and violence of the past, and from the ignorance, fraud, and greed of living men.[38] Thus it was that the wealthy classes had not in the past, and were not now discharging their debt toward society.[39] Such people had profited unduly from the division of social labor; in a thousand ways they enjoyed the fruits of others' toil, adding themselves little or nothing by their own efforts to the common stock. " It is," said Bourgeois, " from these people that I demand the payment of their social debt." [40] So long as these obligations were not discharged, no permanent

37 *Ibid.*, 62.

38 In this it is apparent that Bourgeois relied heavily upon Secrétan.

39 " La solidarité et la liberté," *discussion du rapport, Solidarité, op. cit.*, 108, 109.

40 *Ibid.*, 109.

social contract could exist in France, for class conflicts would continue and society be in danger of disruption. Revolution itself, from Bourgeois' point of view, was to be regarded as nothing more than "the violent repudiation of the social contract." [41]

For these reasons the legislator, without having received any precise mandate from the electorate, was authorized and entitled, thought Bourgeois, to enact reforms that would recall the privileged classes to their sense of social duty and compel them to discharge their social obligations. In assuming this role, public law would but be guaranteeing the permanence, the 'normalness' of quasi-contract. Once however—and this was a crucial point in the solidarist theory—the social balance had been rectified, all were free to follow their inclinations unimpeded by the dictates of the state. Private enterprise, in other words, could continue its operations with a clear conscience once minimum concessions to the working class had been made in the form of poor relief, social insurance, regulation of wage-rates, hours of work, and so forth.

Such was solidarist theory as restated by Bourgeois. It was clearly differentiated from the principal political doctrines current in France at the time. It was, first, distinct from collectivist, or socialist, theory in any form. The aim of *solidarité* was not social equality, the abolition of capitalism, and the inauguration of socialism. *Solidarité* stressed the necessity of maintaining the existing bases of society, of making only those social concessions that would avert the danger of revolution. "The present rights of property," as one writer has succinctly put it, "will be respected on condition that their title holders free themselves from the social debt which they owe toward the community." [42] *Solidarité* was, in fact, a *reformist* theory,

41 "La solidarité et la liberté," *Solidarité, op. cit.*, 91.

42 Louis Deuve, *Étude sur le solidarisme et ses applications économiques* (Paris, 1906), 94. Note also Laski's apt statement that "the revolutionary challenge was to be evaded by the gospel of 'ransom,' a gospel which, in essence, was the notion that wealth must justify its possessors by paying for reasonable amenities for the poor." *The Rise of Liberalism*, (New York, 1936), 275.

not at all a radical one in the sense that it challenged the existing bases of society in the form of private property in capital
or land. Radical only in the sense that it wished to 'soak the
rich' for the financing of the legislative concessions which it
advocated, *solidarité* was thus the philosophic expression of
the program of social reform which the neo-Jacobins, under
pressure of the socialist and trade union organizations, found
it expedient to undertake.

Solidarité was equally clearly differentiated from state socialism. The latter was practised in Germany by Bismarck and
his successors under the form of 'monarchical socialism.' Its
leading advocates, Albert Schäffle in Germany and Dupont-
White in France, stressed the state's role as a paternal authority
guiding economic life and promoting class unity. But Bourgeois
vehemently repudiated the idea that social legislation would
in any way necessarily strengthen the power of the state or
introduce state socialism as practised in Germany. He rejected
the notion that the state should interfere in economic life to
the extent of controlling or regulating the productive process
or the employer-labor relationship. Bourgeois was an antago-
nist of paternalism. He wished to reduce the state to the position of a mere subordinate agency set up to carry out the
decisions made by society and embodied in positive law. Under
no conditions could the state or its legislation be thought of as
"something distinct from men, possessing an authority of its
own by which it would be permitted to impose its terms upon
us." [43] According to this theory law itself was merely a reflection of relations among men, recognizing rights, not creat-
ing them, and providing sanctions for their maintenance.[44] This
theory of law and the state reflected Bourgeois' desire to provide a basis for state intervention in economic life while still
avoiding the idea of paternalism or of a powerful central

43 "La solidarité et la liberté," *discussion du rapport, Solidarité, op. cit.,*
123.

44 *Solidarité, op. cit.,* 43.

authority. It opened the way for the phenomenalist philosophy of law later developed by Duguit.

Most significantly of all, *solidarité* was separated sharply from the traditional Catholic and other Christian doctrines which made charity, or the relief of the poor, a mere matter of *private* morality. To Bourgeois and his party charity was a *public* obligation, and one that could be enforced by law. Whereas, again, traditional ethics conceived of duty as a religious imperative, Bourgeois' doctrine derived it from purely social, or secular sources, preaching performance of obligations in the name of the strong community of interest in society which was alleged to have been produced by the advance of the division of labor. His philosophy thus carried on, into the ethical field, that secular movement which, as has been seen, characterized the entire history of French republicanism. "One must recognize," as one commentator has observed, "that the solidarists do all in their power to break the links between their doctrine and religious traditions. Their work is evidently part of the task undertaken by democracy to laicise ethics themselves." [45]

The advantages of solidarist doctrine for the radicals were obvious. As formulated by Bourgeois this doctrine avoided both the pitfalls of *laissez-faire* liberalism and the commitments of revolutionary socialism; it provided a formula for the amelioration of glaring social abuses while maintaining untouched the existing bases of capitalist society in private property and freedom of business enterprise. It put forth, in terms of the division of labor and men's interdependence, an ideal of social peace and inter-class fraternity designed to mask social conflict, to wean the working class from revolutionary socialism and to win it to support a 'practical' program of social reform. Solidarist doctrine borrowed much from the liberals and the social Darwinists; yet its fundamental debt was still to Rousseau and the Robespierrist Jacobinism of the Great Revolution. "The doctrine of *solidarité*," as Bourgeois claimed,

---

45 Célestin Bouglé, *Le Solidarisme* (in the series *Collection des doctrines politiques*, ed. by André Mater, vol. 4, Paris, 1907), 12, 13.

" appears in the history of ideas as a development of eighteenth century philosophy and as the culmination of the social and political theory to which the Revolution had given the world its first formulation. . . ."[46]

III

The ideas voiced by Bourgeois were not long in finding their way into public circulation. In fact the speed with which they were adopted can be accounted for in no other way than by their timeliness in providing a satisfactory theoretical explanation of current republican practice. The new doctrine was discussed, commented upon, and adopted as a philosophical guide by leading republican intellectuals. It was elaborated in textbooks and expounded in classrooms.[47] *Solidarité* was adopted in the Assembly as " the designated patron of the laws of social hygiene and public assistance."[48] It was the subject of innumerable articles and speeches. By 1914, in effect, *solidarité* had replaced neo-Girondist liberalism as the dominant philosophy of the Third Republic.[49]

Solidarité was launched in intellectual circles by means of a series of conferences held in 1900 and subsequent years. The first of these was the *Congrès international de l'éducation sociale*, held at Paris under government auspices as part of the *Éxposition universelle*.[50] It took place at the *Champ de Mars* at the end of September 1900 and lasted four days. The aim of this meeting was to discuss the concept of *solidarité* and to consider ways and means of diffusing it by education and

46 *Solidarité, op. cit.*, 4.

47 " The greatest enthusiasm was shown for the new doctrine, especially in the universities and among the teachers in a hundred thousand elementary schools." Gide and Rist, *op. cit.*, 593.

48 Bouglé, *Solidarisme* (1924 edition), 7.

49 *Ibid.*, chapter 1, *passim.*

50 The Congress was actually organized by the *Société de l'éducation sociale* which had been formed by a group of radical-socialist intellectuals in 1895.

propaganda throughout the universities and schools. The gathering was attended by many leaders of the Radical and Radical-Socialist Party, and the audience was largely composed of Senators, Deputies, members of the teaching profession, magistrates, industrialists and representatives of trade unions and cooperatives.[51]

Millerand, who was at that time Minister of Commerce in the Waldeck-Rousseau cabinet, presided over the opening session. He indicated the official interest taken in the meeting by remarking that " the government follows with interest an activity whose aim it is to establish social happiness by linking together men's interests with their sympathies." Bourgeois himself was president of the Congress and delivered the opening and closing addresses. Other leading neo-Jacobins who spoke were Charles Seignobos, celebrated historian of the Third Republic and author of a work entitled La Solidarité dans l'histoire; Ferdinand Buisson, well known as a republican educator, historian and publicist;[52] Gustave Geffroy, the radical journalist and close associate of Clemenceau; Charles Gide the economist [53] and Émile Durkheim the well-known sociologist.[54]

At the end of its deliberations the Congress passed a resolution which was a concise statement of the doctrine of solidarité and of its practical implications.[55] Natural solidarity, the resolution stated, was a fact. Social justice would not be achieved until men acknowledged the debt which arose from this mutual interdependence and payment of which was " the essential price of human freedom." The discharge of this obligation would be achieved in three ways, by public education, by insurance

51 Reports of the proceedings of the Congress are contained in Ministère du Commerce et de l'Industrie, Congrès international de l'éducation sociale (1900), procès-verbal sommaire (Paris, 1902); and in Bourgeois, Solidarité, op. cit.

52 See below, 185-186.

53 See below, 184.

54 See below, 183.

55 Procès-verbal sommaire, op cit., 16, 17.

against old age and infirmity, and by insurance against social risks such as industrial accidents and involuntary unemployment.

The *Congrès international* was followed up by a series of lectures under the auspices of the *École des hautes études sociales* in the winters of 1901 to 1902 and 1902 to 1903.[56] The first of these series was delivered, among others, by Bourgeois, Buisson, Gide, and the philosopher Émile Boutroux. A full report of all these meetings and of the discussions that they occasioned was published in 1907 under the title *Essai d'une philosophie de la solidarité.* Little new was added to what had been said at the *Congrès international,* but the leading concepts of solidarist doctrine received further elaboration. The relationship of *solidarité* to socialism, to moral theory, to economic life and social legislation was defined and explored.

The philosophy of *solidarité* had come into existence to explain neo-Jacobin interventionism, but it was soon seen that it could be used to justify many types of state action outside the fields of factory legislation and social insurance. A second series of discussions held in the winter of 1902 to 1903 elaborated upon the many practical applications of solidarist doctrine.[57] The contributors included a number of medical men

56 The *École des hautes études sociales* was founded in 1900 with the purpose, as its statute says, of "organizing the teaching of social science at the higher educational levels." The aim of the School was specifically to teach 'social solidarity' in its application to the current problems of the Third Republic, thus filling a gap in the practice of contemporary higher education. The institution was divided into four departments, dealing respectively with social studies, art, ethics and journalism. Series of courses were given by associated specialists, and discussions organized. The social science department grouped a number of leading republican historians and *savants,* among them Georges Weill, Émile Durkheim, Léon Duguit, Célestin Bouglé, Gabriel Séailles, etc. The president of the School was the liberal philosopher Émile Boutroux. For further details see *L'École des hautes études sociales, 1900-1910* (Paris, 1911).

57 A report of these lectures was published under the title *Les Applications sociales de la solidarité* (Paris, 1904).

and administrators, the best known of whom were Georges Paulet and Henri Monod.[58] In their deliberations it was claimed that the entire field of social legislation—old age, accident, and unemployment insurance, legislation on child welfare, social hygiene, etc.—must be construed as a practical application of the solidarist principle. The state, it was concluded, had an obligation to enforce public health standards and to engage in a fight against infant mortality and tuberculosis.

But the important practical application which was claimed for the principle of *solidarité* lay in the field of legislation governing factory operations and social insurance. In 1898 a law had been passed setting up a comprehensive scheme of insurance against industrial accidents. The solidarists claimed that this measure, as modified by the law of 1902, was " the first great social law of the Third Republic." They insisted that it was a landmark because it gave legal recognition to the principle of collective responsibility, because it enshrined juridically " consciousness of the existence of a social debt that must be paid to men who are living now," [59] and because it indicated the transition " from material and moral to legal solidarity." [60]

In 1903 discussions on *solidarité* were held at the *Académie des sciences morales et politiques*. They followed Charles Brunot's reading of a paper [61] that was a small treatise on *solidarité* and one of the best of many articles that appeared in

58 Georges Paulet was professor at the *École libre des sciences politiques*, and Director of Social Insurance at the Ministry of Commerce; also editor of the *Revue de législation ouvrière et sociale*. Monod was a doctor of medicine and the author of various monographs on public health.

59 Georges Paulet, " La legislation sur les accidents de travail," *Les Applications sociales, op. cit.*, 164.

60 *Ibid.*, 180.

61 " Étude sur la solidarité sociale comme principe des lois," *Séances et travaux de l'Academie* (Vergé), *compte-rendu* CLX (1903, 2ᵉ semestre), 305 ff.

parliamentary and philosophical journals during the course of this one year.[62]

These first discussions and formulations bore fruit subsequently in the form of philosophical texts and expositions. Until 1914 many intellectuals carried on the work of developing *solidarité* and of putting forward a systematic philosophy of interventionism.[63] Solidarist ideas, as previously those of neo-Girondism, began to penetrate the teaching of the social studies and jurisprudence.

The intellectuals were concerned to expound *solidarité* as a physical relationship among men in society, as an ideal of social consciousness, and as a moral and legal theory. As we have noted, the first of these concepts had already been developed in great detail as the result of the work of Spencer, Éspinas and Schäffle. In France in particular the idea of *natural* or organic solidarity had been developed exhaustively by Émile Durkheim.[64] Durkheim in his famous dissertation

62 Other articles and commentaries that may be cited are: Célestin Bouglé, "L'évolution du solidarisme," *Revue politique et parlementaire*, XXXV (1903), 480-505; L. Mirman, "Une loi de solidarité sociale," *ibid.*, xxxvii (1903), 49-73; and Eugène d'Eichthal, "Solidarité sociale et solidarisme," *ibid.*, 97-116.

63 Gide claimed that "there is no such thing as a solidarist school in the sense in which we speak of a Historical, Liberal or a Marxian school." *History of Economic Doctrines, op. cit.*, 601. This position was based upon the contention that the solidarists were a political party with a program of state intervention rather than a group bound together by a common philosophy. But this point seems questionable to the present writer. *Solidarité*, it is true, was a sufficiently nebulous concept to cover various ideological divergences among its many supporters, some of whom rejected Gide's continued advocacy of cooperatives as a panacea for individual misery. *Solidarité* did provide a coherent interventionist philosophy that differentiated the neo-Jacobins from the neo-Girondists on one side and from the *Sansculottes* on the other. As such it constituted a definite school of thought and must be dealt with as such.

64 Émile Durkheim (1858-1917) began to teach sociology at the University of Bordeaux in 1887 where he was a colleague of Alfred Éspinas and Léon Duguit. Durkheim attracted wide attention with his dissertation published in 1893, and subsequently taught at the University of Paris. In 1898 he founded the influential *Année sociologique* of which he was for many years the editor-in-chief. Around this journal he grouped many leading neo-Jacobin *savants*.

published in 1893 on *La Division du travail social* elaborated the idea of a solidarity based upon the division of labor in society that binds men together independently of their own volition and makes them mutually interdependent; and he was, after Fouillée, one of the first French thinkers to make the clear distinction between organic and moral solidarity which was, as we have seen, central to Bourgeois' theory. It was, therefore, to the moral and legal aspects of *solidarité* that attention was primarily given after 1900. Its most important elaborators in the theory of law were Léon Duguit [65] and Joseph Charmont.[66] As a moral and social philosophy it was expounded by numerous writers, among whom Richard,[67] Bouglé,[68] Duprat [69] and Gide [70] were the most eminent.

65 Léon Duguit (1859-1928) spent most of his life as a professor of law at the University of Bordeaux. His work was very influential in developing the anti-statist, pragmatic conception of law which, as we have noted, was an integral part of *solidarité*.

66 Joseph Charmont (1859-1922) was from 1885 professor of civil law at the University of Bordeaux. He presented *solidarité* as a modern version of the older concept of natural law.

67 Gaston Richard (1860- ?) was professor of social science at the University of Bordeaux and the author of numerous works on ethics, social philosophy and the history of political theory. Combining the traditional liberal and the 'organismic' approaches he may be considered one of the ablest continuators of Fouillée's ideas.

68 Célestin Bouglé (1870-1940) began to attract attention just after the turn of the century with works on the theory of democracy and morals. He was director of the *École normale supérieure* and with Durkheim a co-editor of the *Année sociologique*. He edited the collected works of Proudhon and was the author of numerous books on sociology and an influential popularizer of *solidarité*.

69 Guillaume Duprat (1872-) was an exponent of egalitarian democracy and of neo-Jacobin social philosophy. His most important works were *La Solidarité sociale* (Paris, 1907) and *Science sociale et démocratie* (Paris, 1900).

70 Charles Gide (1847-1932) was a professor of political economy at the Universities of Bordeaux and Montpellier. In 1887 he founded the *Revue d'économie politique* to give expression to his cooperatist views. Later he became an important popularizer of *solidarité* of which he considered cooperatism to be a significant expression.

It has become clear from the above examination that *solidarité* developed to no small extent out of previous neo-Girondist thought and that in the final analysis it contested only to a limited degree the ideas of the sanctity of private property and of *laissez-faire* upon which neo-Girondism was based. Toward the end of the nineteenth century a practical demonstration was given of the close relationship between the two philosophies. At that time numerous liberals, impressed by the success of radical-socialism, abandoned the Center to swell the ranks of the neo-Jacobins. Simultaneously they adopted the interventionist philosophy—for campaign purposes at least—and became vociferous exponents of *solidarité*. The prototype and the most influential of these leftward moving neo-Girondists was Ferdinand Buisson (1841-1932). He is worthy of mention here because his life underlines the very real connection, philosophic and political, between the two groups of ideas with which we have hitherto been concerned.

Buisson [71] was the son of a French Protestant magistrate who fled with his family to Switzerland after Napoleon III's *coup d'état* in 1851. He returned to Paris with the outbreak of the Franco-Prussian war in 1870 and remained for many years a close associate of the neo-Girondins. Buisson during this period had strong affinities with the general philosophical and religious position taken by Renouvier and Secrétan. His major interest in life was the development of popular education as an antidote to Catholic influence in the schools, a subject upon which he wrote numerous pamphlets. As an educator he took as his main inspiration Sebastian Castellion, the famous Calvinist teacher, a life of whom he published after twenty years of work in 1892.[72] Buisson himself was one of the main architects of the educational program carried through

---

71 Biographical details will be found in the *Bulletin historique et littéraire de la société de l'histoire du protestantisme français*, LXXXI (1932), 75; in *Le Temps*, February 17 and 18, 1932, and in *La Nouvelle Encyclopédie*.

72 *Sébastien Castellion, sa vie et son œuvre, 1515-1563* (Paris, 1892).

by the opportunists during the early years of the Republic; it was he who, under the direction of Jules Ferry, Paul Bert, and Réné Goblet prepared the various laws, directives, and decrees that gave effect to the new system. He finally left the civil service in 1896 and became professor of education at the Sorbonne.

Toward the end of the nineteenth century Buisson began to shift politically toward the neo-Jacobins, and in 1898 was elected president of the *Ligue pour la défense des droits de l'homme*, a society formed under Clemenceau's inspiration to combat the anti-Dreyfusards. In 1902 he was returned to the Chamber of Deputies and became a leading spokesman for the Radical Party. His work *La Politique radicale* [73] was described by Bourgeois as " a synthesis of our political ideas." It presented a sketch of the evolution of radical-socialism and a detailed statement of the practical aspects of neo-Jacobin interventionism.

The rising strike movement of the early years of the twentieth century and the increasing bitterness of the class conflict in France did not dim the faith of the radicals in *solidarité* as a philosophy of social peace. On the eve of the first great world war this philosophy appeared to be firmly established as the official theory of the *bourgeois* Republic.

73 *Op. cit.*

CONCLUSION

The first and most general conclusion that may be drawn from our study of republican ideas concerns the relation of the latter to the circumstances of their production. It would seem, at first sight, as though ideas originate and develop with a logic that is peculiarly their own and independent of exterior conditioning. Actually, political theory originates from a consideration of highly concrete problems of social life to which the clearest thinkers of an epoch give lucid expression. Various groups adopt concepts that are a reflection of their own problems and position *vis-à-vis* other groups in society. Each group evolves, by a method of trial and error, theoretical syntheses that are primarily applicable to the conditions of the given time and place and are to be comprehended and interpreted in precisely the same limited frame of reference.

Republican theory of the late nineteenth century in France found its leading concepts mainly in the eighteenth century. At that time an outburst of speculation and theorizing prepared and formulated the central ideas with the help of which subsequent republican thought was to build. Republican-democratic thought of the later nineteenth century owes a significant debt of gratitude to the progressive intellectual traditions of the pre-revolutionary era.

The Great Revolution speeded up the formation of republican doctrine and produced the main internal cleavages by which it has ever since been characterized. The three central types of republican thought that appeared after 1789 were mutually antagonistic, but all had in common a boldness and a political radicalism that ran far beyond contemporary opinion and the actualities of the contemporary situation. Many years were to elapse before the French people had convinced themselves through ample and bitter experience that their democratic aspirations could not find satisfaction in a monarchical state.

During the dynastic era which stretched roughly over the first three quarters of the nineteenth century the republican movement was for the most part on the defensive. It produced no very significant amount of what might strictly be termed republican political thought. Nonetheless the reasons for the republican triumph in the last quarter of the nineteenth century and the efflorescence of republican ideas that occurred at that time may be traced in large part to events that had taken place during the earlier period. The dynastic era, in the first place, witnessed an enormous extension of French manufacture and its gradual transformation by machine-power. Masses of people were as a result being pressed into a condition of life which alienated them with increasing force from the more or less authoritarian rule of the various dynasties. The latter had themselves become hopelessly compromised by too close association with one or other element in the small, rich clique which comprised the true and effective rulers of France in this epoch. As a result the dynasties remained isolated from the people, were unable to demonstrate their value as national rather than class governments and failed totally to satisfy the democratic sentiments and aspirations of the masses. Their eventual collapse was thus assured.[1] The dynastic era, in the second place, produced a mass of speculation which later thinkers were to draw upon heavily, and from this point of view that era has an importance in French intellectual history ranking second only to the eighteenth century itself. Republicanism though actually weak at the time was able to profit by the long period of gestation which placed at its disposal the socialist speculations which were the direct result of the changes in social conditions which industrialism was generating. It may therefore be seen that by 1870 not only were the conditions ripe but the material was at hand out of which mature formulations of the republican position could be produced.

1 It was hastened after the *debâcle* of 1870 by the fact that the dynasties in addition to being isolated from the people were also deeply divided among themselves.

After the collapse of dynastic power, accordingly, republican thought moved rapidly forward. Until the outbreak of the first World War this type of theorizing was both plentiful and varied. It tackled many of the central problems of national life and attracted some of the best thinkers which the French schools could boast. Its concepts and formulae were applied to all the social studies and stimulated activity that produced an elaborate, highly developed and many-sided republican ideology.

The two republican schools of thought which became in succession both practically and theoretically dominant in France between 1870 and 1914 were closely related and at the same time fundamentally contrasted. Both neo-Girondism and neo-Jacobinism were clearly affiliated to traditions and concepts which had been produced during an earlier period, at the time of the Great Revolution. Both adhered to the ideas of private property, of the sacredness of human rights and of parliamentary democracy as enshrined in the republican state. Both drew heavily upon the social thought of the eighteenth century and of the new industrial age for theories by means of which to reconcile or to exorcize class conflicts and to reinforce the unity of the republican regime. Both were directly opposed to *Sansculotte* theories of socialist republicanism which was based upon the denial of private property and of the rights connected with it.

But neo-Girondism and neo-Jacobinism differed markedly with regard to the social orientation of their supporters. Neo-Jacobinism was far more " popular " than the essentially aristocratic theory of its rival. As opposed to the latter its primary appeal was to the *petite bourgeoisie* and to all those identified with that class. It appealed secondarily and for a limited period to the working people for the satisfaction of whose immediate interests it was led to develop the idea of a " welfare state " which, limited and tentative as it was, yet went far beyond the potentialities of the neo-Girondist *laissez-faire* ideal.

Neo-Jacobinism was indebted to neo-Girondism for many of its ideas, evolved out of it and finally supplanted it as the dominant philosophy of the French republican state. It reproduced the leading concepts of neo-Girondism but in a new context that stressed action by the state and state concessions to the interests of factory workers, invalids, the aged and unemployed. This evolution of republican philosophy reflected changes that were currently taking place in political and social relationships. It measured the extent to which republicans considered state " interference " compatible with the maintenance of the traditional liberal republican ideal.

The two schools, finally, were contrasted with respect to their inner unity as systems of thought. Neo-Jacobinism in the form of *solidarité* was a clearly unified system, but within neo-Girondism important and fundamental divergences existed. These were in themselves a reflection of the confusion and uncertainty that accompanied the years during which the Third Republic was inaugurated.

Those neo-Girondists who were convinced of the necessity and inevitability of republican victory were, for the most part, numbered among the followers of Renouvier. His neo-Kantian philosophy provided reasons for believing that political, republican democracy was *per se* superior to any other kind of regime and that good men were morally obliged to strive for progress in that direction. Those neo-Girondists, on the other hand, who like their revolutionary forbears entertained doubts about the wisdom of instituting a democratic republic and at times allowed their fears to get the better of them, were numbered among the followers of Littré. Littré no less than Renouvier had a theory of progress, but it was not nearly so closely allied with republicanism. He and his followers were in fact empiricists who permitted themselves the cautious conclusion that, on inspection, the *bourgeois* republic was the most practical means for the achievement of their goals of industrial development and of individual enrichment. Of the two modes of thought Renouvier's proved much the more tenacious of life. Littré's sociological republicanism either disintegrated after his death or was kept alive, in the hands of Émile Faguet, only at the cost of a complete change of inner content and meaning.

No such clear divergences may be found among the neo-Jacobins as among the neo-Girondists. The differences that existed between Clemenceau, the practical advocate of state interventionism, and the more theoretical exponents of *solidarité*, were of a different order. Clemenceau won support among the French peasantry and working people as a politician who was, during the earlier period of his career, committed to a strenuous defense of the Republic and to the advocacy of measures of social reform designed to alleviate the worst evils of industrial life. The concessions subsequently made by the *bourgeois* state in the form of welfare legislation became the basis for the elaboration by theorists like Fouillée of a comprehensive philosophy of social reform. Clemenceau's championing of social legislation and Léon Bourgeois' *solidarité* corresponded to two different periods in the evolution of the Radical and Radical Socialist Party. Each formulation was, at the time when made, an appropriate expression of the fundamental objectives of neo-Jacobinism.

The republican thought of the late nineteenth century is valuable primarily as an aid in mastering the general history and the political life of the epoch. The schools of thought that we have dealt with here retained some of their vitality after the close of our period but in the years between the two World Wars they declined considerably in importance. Indeed the closing years of the Third Republic produced abundant evidence that both types of thought would soon be superseded by *Sansculotte* republican ideologies. The development of the latter into a uniquely French type of socialist republican thought is clearly a story in itself. But this much we may safely say, such thought is indebted to the same liberal and revolutionary traditions as the rest of republican thought but evolves in direct contrast to the latter and as its antithesis. The present essay may then have served the purpose of defining *Sansculotte* thought as it were negatively, in terms of its opposites. Thereby it will perhaps provide a link with a significant chapter of French intellectual history which yet remains to be written.

BIBLIOGRAPHY

A. General

Bibliographies. The two aids that have been found most useful in the preparation of the present essay are: (1) *Catalogue général des livres imprimés de la Bibliothèque Nationale* (Paris, 1897-1947). This great reference work is still incomplete, but may be consulted for all works printed in France up to 1936. A *Supplément* to this catalogue is available at the *Bibliothèque Nationale* for all works published during the years 1937 to the present. (2) A. Grandin, *Bibliographie générale des sciences juridiques, politiques, économiques, et sociales: 1800-1925*, 3 vols. (Paris, 1925). Fifteen supplementary volumes bring this valuable reference work up to date for the years 1926-1945 inclusive.

Specialized bibliographies for the works of writers dealt with in this essay are indicated in the footnotes.

Periodicals and newspapers. These sources are listed under B. below in the appropriate place. Wherever it has seemed desirable they have been described more fully either in the text or in footnotes. For guidance in the complex maze of French journalism two of the most helpful guides are the periodical catalogue of the *Bibliothèque Nationale* and the *Annuaire de la presse française.*

Biography. A word may usefully be said about sources for biographical information, for the problem of obtaining full and accurate information about French thinkers, writers and statesmen of the early Third Republic is not by any means a minor one. As aids to biographical research I have found the following to be the most helpful sources and guides: (1) The *Catalogue de biographie française* of the *Bibliothèque Nationale.* This guide is not complete and it is certainly not up-to-date, but it gives valuable indications of available biographical information for a large number of people. (2) *La Grande Encyclopédie* (Paris, n. d.). This work is a valuable source for the biography of nineteenth century France up to shortly before the first World War. (3) *Polybiblion.* Described as a " revue bibliographique universelle," this periodical has been published monthly since 1868. Its main purpose has been to review new books, but it has also contained valuable biographical material in the form of obituaries. (4) Georges Vapereau, editor: *Dictionnaire universel des contemporains* (Paris, 1876). This work, in its various editions up to 1893, is not without value, but gives only the scantiest attention to most republicans. (5) *Grand Dictionnaire universel du 19ᵉ siècle* (Paris, 1928-1933). Gives brief but reliable information about a great many people.

B. Topical

The following is a selected list, arranged by topics, of the printed material found most useful in the preparation of this essay. It is not intended to be a comprehensive bibliography of the subjects dealt with.

I. THE HISTORY OF THE THIRD REPUBLIC, 1870-1914 [1]

Acomb, Evelyn M. *The French Laic Laws (1879-1899)*. New York, 1941.

Benoit-Lévy, Edmond. *Histoire de quinze ans, 1870-1885*. Paris, 1885.

Bourgin, Georges. *La Troisième République*. Paris, 1939.

——. *La Guerre de 1870-1871 et la Commune*. Paris, 1939.

Brabant, Frank H. *The Beginnings of the Third Republic in France, a History of the National Assembly, February-September, 1871*. London, 1940.

Brogan, D. W. *France under the Republic: the Development of Modern France, 1870-1939*. New York, 1941.

Deluns-Montaud. "La philosophie de Gambetta." In the *Revue politique et parlementaire*, XI (1897).

Farmer, Paul. *France Reviews its Revolutionary Origins*. New York, 1944.

Favre, Léopold. *Histoire politique de l'année 1877*. Niort, 1878.

Goguel, François. *La Politique des partis sous la Troisième République*. Paris, 1946.

Hale, Richard W. *Democratic France: the Third Republic from Sedan to Vichy*. New York, 1941.

Jacques, Léon. *Les Partis politiques sous la Troisième République*. Paris, 1913.

Leyret, Henry. *Waldeck-Rousseau et la Troisième République*. Paris, 1908.

Louis, Paul. *Histoire du socialisme en France*. Paris, 1946.

Seignobos, Charles. *Le Déclin de l'Empire et l'établissement de la Troisième République (1859-1875)*. In the series *Histoire de la France contemporaine depuis le Révolution jusqu'à la paix de 1919*, edited by Ernest Lavisse, vol. 7. Paris, 1921.

——. *L'Évolution de la Troisième République (1875-1914)*. Vol. 8 of the same series. Paris, 1921.

Sibert, Marcel. *La Constitution de la France*. Paris, 1946.

Soulier, A. *L'Instabilité ministérielle sous la Troisième République (1871-1938)*. Paris, 1939.

Thomson, David. *Democracy in France: the Third Republic*. New York, 1946.

Vidal, J. *Le Mouvement ouvrier français de la Commune à la Guerre Mondiale (aperçu historique)*. Paris, 1934.

Winnacker, R. A. "The Third French Republic, 1870-1914." In the *Journal of Modern History*, X (1938).

Zévaès, Alexandre. *Histoire de la Troisième République. Nouvelle édition complétée et augmentée*. Paris, 1946.

——. *Histoire du socialisme et du communisme en France de 1871 a 1947*. Paris, 1947.

——. *De l'introduction du Marxisme en France*. Paris, 1947.

[1] A comprehensive bibliography of the history of the Third Republic during this period is provided in Winnacker's article cited below. Most of the works here cited have either appeared subsequently or were omitted from Winnacker's list.

2. FRENCH REPUBLICAN IDEAS AND THE LIBERAL TRADITION

Advielle, Victor. *Histoire de Gracchus Babeuf et du babouvisme d'après de nombreux documents inédits.* 2 vols. Paris, 1884.

Aulard, Alphonse. *The French Revolution, 1789-1804.* 4 vols. London, 1910.

——. *Christianity and the French Revolution.* London, 1927.

Baird, H. M. *The Huguenots and the Revocation of the Edict of Nantes.* 2 vols. 1895.

Becker, Carl. *The Heavenly City of the Eighteenth Century Philosophers.* New Haven, 1932.

Bryce, James. *Modern Democracies.* 2 vols. New York, 1921.

Clapham, J. H. *The Economic Development of France and Germany, 1815-1914.* Cambridge, 1928.

Coker, F. W. *Recent Political Thought.* New York, 1934.

Dodge, Guy Howard. *The Political Theory of the Huguenots of the Dispersion.* New York, 1947.

Fabre, Joseph. *Les Pères de la Révolution de Bayle à Condorcet.* Paris, 1910.

Fisher, H. A. L. *The Republican Tradition in Europe.* New York, 1911.

Gottschalk, L. " Studies since 1920 of French thought in the period of the Enlightenment." *Journal of Modern History,* IV (1932).

Guérin, Daniel. *La Lutte de classes sous la Première République: bourgeois et bras nus (1793-1797).* 2 vols. Paris, 1946.

Hattersley, Alan F. *A Short History of Democracy.* Cambridge, 1930.

Hearnshaw, F. J. C., editor. *Social and Political Ideas of some great French Thinkers of the Age of Reason.* London, 1930.

Jaurès, Jean. *Histoire socialiste de la Révolution française.* Mathiez edition, 4 vols. Paris, 1939.

Lecky, W. E. H. *History of the Rise and Influence of the Spirit of Rationalism in Europe.* London, 1904.

Lichtenberger, André. *Le Socialisme au 18ᵉ siècle.* Paris 1895.

Martin, Germain. *Histoire économique et financière.* In the series *Histoire de la nation française,* edited by Gabriel Hanotaux, vol. X. Paris, 1927.

Martin, Kingsley. *French Liberal Thought in the Eighteenth Century: a study of political ideas from Bayle to Condorcet.* London, 1929.

Mathiez, Albert. *La Révolution française.* 3 vols. Paris, 1948.

——. *La Vie chère et le mouvement social sous la Terreur.* Paris, 1927.

——. *Girondins et Montagnards.* Paris, 1930.

Merriam, Charles Edward, and Harry Elmer Barnes, editors. *A History of Political Theory (Recent Times).* New York, 1924.

Meslier, Jean. *Le Testament de Jean Meslier.* 3 vols. Amsterdam, 1864.

Montesquieu. *Œuvres complètes.* 7 vols. Paris, 1875-1879.

Morelly, L'Abbé. *Code de la nature.* Paris, 1841.

Mornet, Daniel. *French Thought in the Eighteenth Century.* New York, 1929.

Muret, Charlotte T. *French Royalist Doctrines since the Revolution.* New York, 1933.

Roucek, Joseph S., editor. *Twentieth Century Political Thought.* New York, 1946.

Roustan, Marius. *Les Philosophes et la société française au 18ᵉ siècle.* Lyon, 1906.

Ruggiero, Guido. *A History of European Liberalism.* London, 1927.

Schapiro, S. J. *Condorcet and the Rise of Liberalism.* New York, 1934.

Sée, Henri. *Les Idées politiques en France au 17ᵉ siècle.* Paris, 1923.

——. *L'Évolution de la pensée politique en France au 18ᵉ siècle.* Paris, 1925.

——. *Esquisse d'une histoire économique et sociale de la France.* Paris, 1927.

Sencier, Georges. *Le Babouvisme après Babeuf. (Sociétés secrètes et conspirations communistes, 1830-1848).* Paris, 1912.

Siegfried, André. *Tableau des partis en France.* Paris, 1930.

Soltau, Roger H. *French Political Thought in the Nineteenth Century.* New Haven, 1931.

Tchernoff, I. *Le Parti républicain en France sous la monarchie de Juillet: formation et évolution de la doctrine républicaine.* Paris, 1901.

——. *Le Parti républicain au coup d'état et sous le second Empire.* Paris, 1906.

Turgot, Anne. *Œuvres de Turgot.* 2 vols. Paris, 1844.

Vaughan, C. E., editor. *The Political Writings of Jean-Jacques Rousseau.* 2 vols. Cambridge, 1915.

Voltaire. *Œuvres complètes de Voltaire.* New edition, conformable to Beuchot, 25 vols. Paris, 1879.

Weill, Georges. *Histoire du parti républicain en France.* Paris, 1900.

Weulersse, G. *Les Physiocrates.* Paris, 1931.

3. RENOUVIER AND PHILOSOPHIC LIBERALISM

Boas, G. *French Philosophies of the Romantic Period.* Baltimore, 1925.

Bouglé, C. "Une doctrine idéaliste de la démocratie: l'œuvre de Henry Michel." *Revue politique et parlementaire,* XLIII (1905).

Cornwell, Irène. *Les Principes du droit dans la philosophie de Charles Renouvier.* Paris, 1922.

Foucher, Louis. *La Jeunesse de Renouvier.* Paris, 1927.

Hamelin, O. *Le Système de Renouvier.* Paris, 1927.

James, Henry, editor. *The Letters of William James.* Boston, 1926.

Lafargue, Paul. "La Participation," *Égalité,* April 16, 23, and 30, 1882.

Lévy-Bruhl, Lucien. *History of Modern Philosophy in France.* Chicago, 1924.

Marion, François-Henri. *De la solidarité morale.* Paris, 1880.

Michel, Henry. *Le Quarantième Fauteuil.* Paris, 1898.

——. *L'Idée de l'État.* Paris, 1895.

——. *La Doctrine politique de la démocratie.* Paris, 1901.

——. *Notes sur l'enseignement secondaire.* Paris, 1902.

——. *Edgar Quinet: conférence faite à université populaire de Lyon.* Lyon, 1903.

——. *Propos de morale.* 3 vols. Paris, 1904-1905.

——. *La Loi Falloux.* Paris, 1906.

Mouy, P. *L'Idée de progrès dans la philosophie de Renouvier.* Paris, 1927.

Picard, Roger. *La Philosophie sociale de Renouvier.* Paris, 1908.

Pillon, François. *La Philosophie de Charles Secrétan.* Paris, 1898.

Prat, Louis. *Charles Renouvier, philosophe: sa doctrine, sa vie.* Pamiers, 1937.

Ravaisson-Mollien, Félix. *La Philosophie en France au 19° siècle.* Paris, 1868.

Renouvier, Charles. *Manuel républicain de l'homme et du citoyen.* Ed. J. Thomas. Paris, 1904.

——. *Organization communale et centrale de la République.* Paris, 1851.

——. *Essais de critique générale.* 4 vols. Paris, 1854-1864.

——. *Science de la morale.* 2 vols. Paris, 1869.

——. *Uchronie (l'utopie dans l'histoire) : ésquisse historique du developpement de la société européenne, tel qu'il n'a pas été, tel qu'il aurait pu être.* Paris, 1876.

——. *Philosophie analytique de l'histoire.* 4 vols. Paris, 1896-1898.

——. *Les Derniers Entretiens.* Set down in writing by Louis Prat. Paris, 1904.

Renouvier, Charles, and François Pillon, editors. *La Critique philosophique.* Paris, 1872-1889.

Renouvier, Charles, and Charles Secrétan. *Correspondance de Renouvier et Secrétan.* Paris, 1910.

Richard, Gaston. *La Question sociale et le mouvement philosophique au 19° siècle.* Paris, 1914.

Séailles, Georges. *La Philosophie de Charles Renouvier.* Paris, 1905.

Secrétan, Charles. *La Philosophie de la liberté.* Paris, 1866.

——. *Études sociales.* Lausanne, 1889.

——. *La Civilization et la croyance.* Paris, 1892.

——. *Mon utopie: nouvelles étudies morales et sociales.* Paris, 1892.

Secrétan, Louise. *Charles Secrétan, sa vie et son œuvre.* 4th ed. Paris, 1912.

Verneaux, R. *Renouvier, disciple et critique de Kant.* Paris, 1945.

Weill, Georges. *Histoire de l'idée laique en France au 19° siècle.* Paris, 1929.

4. ÉMILE LITTRÉ AND REPUBLICAN SOCIOLOGY

Belis, A. *La Critique française à la fin du 19° siècle.* Laroche-sur-Yon, 1926.

Bloch, Maurice. *Les Mères des grands hommes.* Paris, 1885.

Bordeaux, Henri. *Pèlerinages littéraires.* Paris, 1905.

Caro, E. "Émile Littré." In the *Revue des deux mondes*, L (1882).

——. *M. Littré et le positivisme.* Paris, 1883.

Daremberg, Georges. *Les Grande Médecins du 19ᵉ siècle.* Paris, 1907.

Desjardins, Arthur. *Questions sociales et politiques.* Paris, 1893.

——. *De la liberté politique dans l'état moderne.* Paris, 1894.

Duval, Maurice. *Émile Faguet: le critique, le moraliste, le sociologue.* Paris, 1911.

Faguet, Émile. *Politiques et moralistes du 19ᵉ siècle.* 3 vols. Paris, 1891-1899.

——. *La Patrie.* In the series *Les Dix Commandements.* Paris, n. d.

——. "Sur les idées maitresses de la Révolution." In *L'Œuvre sociale de la Révolution française.* Paris, n. d.

——. *Questions politiques.* 2nd edition. Paris, 1902.

——. *Problèmes politiques du temps présent.* 4th edition. Paris, 1904.

——. *L'Anticléricalisme.* Paris, 1906.

——. *Le Socialisme en 1907.* Paris, 1907.

——. *Discussions politiques.* Paris, 1909.

——. *La Démission de la morale.* Paris, 1910.

——. *Le Culte de l'incompétence.* Paris, 1910.

——. *Et l'horreur des responsabilités.* Paris, 1911.

——. *Le Libéralisme.* Paris, 1912.

——. *Rousseau penseur.* Paris, 1912.

——. *De l'idée de patrie: discours prononcé à la distribution des prix du lycée Janson-de-Sailly, le 12 Juillet, 1913.* Paris, 1913.

Ferraz, Marin. *Socialisme, naturalisme, positivisme.* Being vol. I of *L'Histoire de la philosophie en France au 19ᵉ siècle.* 4th edition, augmented. Paris, 1882.

Giraud, Victor. *Écrivains et soldats.* Paris, 1921.

Littré, Émile. *Conservation, révolution, positivisme.* Paris, 1852.

——. *Ibid.* 2nd edition. 1879.

——. *Paroles de philosophie positive.* Paris, 1863.

——. "Quelques mots de préambule." In *Ce qu'est le socialisme,* by Felix Aroux. Paris, 1870.

——. *Restauration de la legitimité et des ses alliés.* Paris, 1873.

——. *Fragments de philosophie positive et de sociologie contemporaine.* Paris, 1876.

——. *De l'établissement de la Troisième République.* Paris, 1880.

Littré, Émile, editor. *La Philosophie positive.* Paris, 1867-1883.

Polybiblion. "Émile Littré." 2ᵉ série. XIII (1881).

——. "Émile Faguet." 2ᵉ série. LXXXIV (1916).

Sainte-Beuve, Charles. *Notice sur M. Littré, sa vie et ses travaux.* Paris, 1863.

Séché, Alphonse. *Émile Faguet.* Paris, 1904.

Seillière, Ernest. *Émile Faguet.* Paris, 1938.

Spuller, Eugène. *Figures disparues.* 3 vols. Paris, 1886-1894.

Vacherot, Étienne. *La Démocratie.* Paris, 1860.

——. *La Démocratie liberale.* Paris, 1892.

5. CLEMENCEAU AND THE RADICAL REPUBLICANS

This chapter has been based principally upon Clemenceau's speeches and addresses in the period 1876 to 1893. These have not as yet been collected and published in book form. Accordingly the most important of them are set forth here. For public speeches, the date of delivery and the date of publication are both given. For parliamentary addresses the date of delivery only is given. These addresses may be consulted either in the *Journal officiel* or the *Débats parlementaires* in the issue immediately succeeding the date of delivery. A speech delivered, for example, on June 19, 1883 will appear in the issue of the *Débats* dated June 20.

Public Speeches

Nov. 29, 1875. Inaugural address as President of the Paris Municipal Council. Original draft at the *Musée Clemenceau.*

May 12, 1879. Report to his electors at the *Cirque Fernando.* Digest published in *La République française,* May 13, 1879.

April 11, 1880. Report to his electors (*Cirque Fernando*). Published in full in *La Justice,* April 13, 1880.

Oct. 28, 1880. Speech at Marseilles. Published in *La Justice,* Nov. 1, 1880.

Aug. 12, 1881. Report to his electors (*Cirque Fernando*). Published in *La Justice,* Aug. 15, 1881.

Oct. 30, 1882. Report to his electors (*Cirque Fernando*). Published in *La Justice,* Nov. 1, 1882.

May 20, 1883. Speech at Lille. Published in *La Justice,* May 23, 1883.

May 25, 1884. Report to his electors. Published in *La Justice,* May 27, 1884.

July 19, 1885. Speech at Bordeaux. Published in *La Justice,* July 21, 1885.

Sept. 13, 1885. Report to his electors at Draguignan. Published in *La Justice,* Sept. 17, 1885.

Aug. 8, 1893. Speech at Salernes. Published in *La Justice,* Aug. 10, 1893.

Parliamentary Addresses

Clemenceau's numerous speeches on foreign and colonial policy have not been included in the following selected list.

(1) *Labor.* Amnesty for the *Communards,* May 16, 1876 and December 16, 1879. Liberation of Auguste Blanqui, January 21, May 27, and June 3, 1879. Strike of the Gard miners, March 10, 1882. Trade union organization, June 19, 1883. The social question, February 1, 1884. The Anzin strike, April 8, 1884. Defense of Paul Lafargue, October 31, 1891. Pas-de-Calais strike, November 19, 1891. Carmaux strike, November 10, 1892.

(2) *Democratic Rights.* The right of demonstration, May 28, 1880. Freedom of the press, January 24, February 1 and 4, 1881. Freedom of meeting, March 31, 1881. Education, July 10, 1885. Laicizing the state, June 8, 1889.

(3) *Constitutional and Administrative.* Revision of the Constitution, May 31 and November 15, 1881, March 6, 1883, August 13, 1884. Reform of the magistrature, January 22, 1883.

A list of additional material used in the preparation of this chapter follows.

Ajalbert, Jean. *Clemenceau.* Lagny, 1931.

Bruun, Geoffrey. *Clemenceau.* Cambridge (Massachusetts), 1944.

Bure, Émile. " Clemenceau et la Commune." *Revue hebdomadaire* (April, 1930).

Clemenceau, Georges. *American Reconstruction, 1865-1870.* New York, 1928.

——. *Rapport présenté à la commission d'enquête parlementaire sur la situation des ouvriers de l'agriculture et de l'industrie en France (Grève d'Anzin).* Paris, 1885.

——. *La Mêlée sociale.* Paris, 1895.

——. *Les Plus Forts.* Paris, 1898.

——. *Figures de Vendée.* Paris, 1930.

——. *Les Plus Belles Pages.* Paris, 1908.

——. *Aux ambuscades de la vie.* Paris, 1903.

Compère-Morel. *La Question agraire et le socialisme en France.* Paris, 1912.

Daudet, Léon. *Clemenceau.* New York, 1940.

Ducray, Camille. *Clemenceau.* Paris, 1918.

Geffroy, Gustave. *Clemenceau.* Paris, 1919.

Hyndman, H. M. *Clemenceau.* New York, 1919.

Jackson, J. Hampden. *Clemenceau.* London, 1948.

Judet, Ernest. *Clemenceau.* Paris, 1920.

Lafargue, Paul. *Critiques littéraires.* Paris, 1936.

Martet, Jean, editor. *M. Clemenceau peint par lui-même.* Paris, 1929.

——. *Le Silence de M. Clemenceau.* Paris, 1929.

——. *Le Tigre.* Paris, 1930.

Michon, Georges. *Clemenceau.* Paris, 1931.

Mordacq, Jean. *Clemenceau.* Paris, 1939.

Pratt, Julius W. " Clemenceau and Gambetta, a study in Political Philosophy." In the *South Atlantic Quarterly*, XX (1921).

Scize, Pierre. *Georges Clemenceau.* Lyon, 1944.

Zévaès, Alexandre. *Jules Guesde.* Paris, 1928.

Zuckerkandl, Berta S. *Clemenceau tel que je l'ai connu.* Alger, 1945.

6. SOLIDARITÉ

Andler, Charles. " Du quasi-contrat social et de M. Léon Bourgeois." *Revue de métaphysique et de morale*, V (1897).

Bouglé, Célestin. " L'Évolution du solidarisme." *Revue politique et parlementaire*, XXXV (1903).

——. *Le Solidarisme.* In the series *Collection des doctrines politiques*, edited by André Mater, vol. IV. Paris, 1907.

Bourgeois, Léon. *La Solidarité.* 7th edition. Paris, 1912.

Bourgeois, Léon, *et al. Essai d'une philosophie de la solidarité.* Paris, 1907.

——. *Les Applications sociales de la solidarité.* Paris, 1904.

Brunot, Charles. "Étude sur la solidarité sociale comme principe des lois." *Académie des sciences morales et politiques: compte-rendu.* CLX (1903, *2ᵉ semestre*).

——. "Solidarité et charité." *Revue politique et parlementaire.* XXVIII (1901).

Buisson, Ferdinand. *La Politique radicale.* In the series *Collections des doctrines politiques,* edited by André Mater, vol. V. Paris, 1908.

——. *Sébastien Castéllion, sa vie et son oeuvre, 1515-1563.* Paris, 1892.

Charpentier, Armand. *Le Parti radical et radical-socialiste à travers ses congrès.* Paris, 1912.

Deuve, Louis. *Étude sur le solidarisme et ses applications économiques.* Paris, 1906.

Durkheim, Émile. *De la division du travail social.* Translated by George Simpson as *The Division of Labor in Society.* New York, 1933.

d'Eichthal, Eugène. "Solidarité sociale et solidarisme." *Revue politique et parlementaire.* XXXVII (1903).

Éspinas, Alfred. *Des sociétés animales.* Paris, 1877.

Fouillée, Alfred. *La Science sociale contemporaine.* 3rd edition. Paris, 1885.

——. *La Proprieté sociale et la démocratie.* Paris, 1884.

——. *Le Socialisme et la sociologie reformiste.* Paris, 1909.

——. *La Démocratie politique et sociale en France.* Paris, 1910.

Gide, Charles, and Charles Rist. *A History of Economic Doctrines.* Boston, n. d.

Guyau, Augustin. *La Philosophie et la sociologie d'Alfred Fouillée.* Paris, 1913.

Hamburger, M. *Hommes politiques. Léon Bourgeois, 1851-1925.* Paris, 1932.

Jay, Raoul. *La Protection légale des travailleurs.* Paris, 1910.

L'École des hautes études sociales, 1900-1910. Paris, 1911.

Ministère de Commerce et de l'Industrie. Congrès internationale de l'éducation sociale (1900) : *procès-verbal sommaire.* Paris, 1902.

Mirman, L. "Une loi de solidarité sociale." *Revue politique et parlementaire.* XXXVII (1903).

Pic, Paul. *Traité élémentaire de législation industrielle.* Paris, 1894.

——. *Les Assurances sociales en France et à l'étranger.* Paris, 1913.

Schäffle, Albert. *Bau und Leben des sozialen Körpers.* Tübingen, 1875.

Spencer, Arthur W., editor. *Modern French Legal Philosophy.* In the *Modern Legal Philosophy series,* vol 7. Boston, 1916.

INDEX

Absolutism, French, *see* Monarchy, French
Académie des sciences morales et politiques, 182
Adam, Mme. Juliette, 52 n.
Alliance socialiste républicaine, 155
Allier, Raoul, 84 n.
Alsace-Lorraine, 138
  annexation of in 1871, 137
Amedée, Jacques, 54 n.
Ancien Régime, 23, 28, 58, 99
Année philosophique, 54 n.
Anticlericalism, 57, 103, 141
  see also Renouvier, Clemenceau, etc.
  of the Enlightenment, 51
  of Montesquieu, 22
  of the republican movement, 16, 19
Association, Right of, 142-143
  definition of, 142 n.
  labor's demand for, 146

Babeuf, François Noel, 29
  and *Sansculotte* ideal, 39-40
Bayle, Pierre
  and freedom of thought, 23
  and religious persecution, 24
Becker, Carl, 20 n.
Belleville Program, 49
Benthamite Utilitarianism, 171
Bergson, Henri, 160
Bert, Paul, 186
Beudant, Charles, 77
Bible, 23, 71
Bismarck, Otto von, 129, 137-139, 177
  releases French troops to quell *Communards*, 130
Blanc, Louis, 43. 59 n., 70, 85
Blanqui, Auguste, 43, 148
Bonaparte, Louis Napoleon, 41, 47, 61, 64, 98, 127, 132
  capitulation of at Sedan, 129
  coup d'état (1851) of, 54, 90, 185
Bonaparte, Napoleon, 72
  coup d'état (1799) of, 40
Bonapartism, 100, 145
  social roots of, 100 n.
Bonapartists, 131
Bordeaux Assembly, *see* National Assembly
Bouglé, Célestin, 184
Boulanger, General, 170
  and Clemenceau, 134, 149
  and revision of the Constitution, 147

Boulangist Movement, 134-135, 147, 157
  financed by royalists, 134
Bourbon Regime (1815-1830), *see* Restoration, French
Bourgeois, Léon, 80, 163, 169-179, 181, 184, 186, 191
  constitutes himself a leading spokesman of *solidarité*, 170-171
  elaborates idea of social debt as basis of state juridical obligation, 175-176
  and 'natural solidarity' as a social principle, 171-172
  political career of, 169-170
  president of the *Congrés internationale de l'éducation sociale*, 180
  and theory of the social contract, 173-174
Boutroux, Émile, 181
Bretagne, Jacques, 19
Brissot, Jacques, 35
Brochard, Victor, 76
Broglie, Victor de, 47
Brunot, Charles
  and *solidarité*, 182
Bryce, James, 18
Buisson, Ferdinand, 180, 181, 185-186
  affinities with Renouvier and the opportunists, 185, 186
  life of, 185-186
  as spokesman for the Radical Party, 186
Burke, Edmund, 114

Calvinism, French
  and popular education, 71
Castellion, Sebastian, 185
Charmont, Joseph, 184
Carnot, Lazare, 37
Carnot, Hippolyte, 53
Catholicism, 22, *see also* Church of France
Chaumette, Gaspard, 39 n.
Church of France, 16, 19, 20, 29, 49, 50, 57, 71, 75, 89, 94-96 *passim*, 119, 127, 144, 147, 152
  as authoritarian force, 72
  disestablishment of, 25, 73, 102, 103-104, 133, 141-143
  mainstay of French royalism, 49
  under the old regime, 16
  and popular education, 71-72
  and the republican movement, 16